AVERY LOCKE

ASP.NET core web API with Angular

Contents

Introduction

Understanding the Power of Full-Stack Development

In the world of modern software development, the term "full-stack" refers to the development of both front-end (client-side) and back-end (server-side) parts of a web application. Full-stack developers are those who possess the skills and knowledge to work on all layers of a web application, from creating user interfaces and handling client interactions to managing databases, business logic, and application infrastructure.

The rise of full-stack development reflects the industry's need for more versatile and efficient approaches to building applications. Traditionally, software teams have been segmented into specialists, with front-end developers focusing on user experience and design, while back-end developers concentrated on databases, servers, and application logic. However, as technology evolved, so did the demand for developers capable of building and managing entire applications from top to bottom, eliminating the need for constant coordination between different teams and reducing bottlenecks in the development process.

The main advantage of full-stack development is its flexibility. Full-stack developers can jump into any part of a project at any stage, making them valuable assets to a development team. This versatility helps streamline the development process and enables teams to build faster, more cohesive applications without the delays often caused by miscommunication or misunderstandings between front-end and back-end teams.

Moreover, full-stack development allows for a more integrated and seamless product design. When a single developer or team handles both the front-end and back-end development, they can better ensure that the two components work in harmony, resulting in a more efficient and fluid user experience. This alignment between the user interface and the underlying data architecture is crucial for building applications that are not only functional but also scalable, maintainable, and user-friendly.

In full-stack development, the ability to "speak the language" of both sides of the stack is invaluable. Developers can take full responsibility for the user experience while also ensuring that server-side logic and data handling are optimized. In other words, full-stack development fosters a holistic understanding of how web applications operate, making it a powerful approach for building applications that are more cohesive and aligned with both business and user goals.

For those looking to master full-stack development, a combination of ASP.NET Core (a popular back-end framework) and Angular (a powerful front-end framework) offers a robust solution for building dynamic, scalable, and efficient web applications.

Why ASP.NET Core and Angular?

Choosing the right technology stack is one of the most crucial decisions in web development. With countless frameworks, libraries, and tools available, it's essential to select a combination that ensures productivity, scalability, security, and maintainability. ASP.NET Core and Angular are two of the most powerful frameworks in the web development space, and together, they provide an excellent foundation for full-stack development.

ASP.NET Core: A Robust Back-End Framework

ASP.NET Core is a high-performance, open-source, cross-platform framework for building modern web applications. Developed by Microsoft, ASP.NET Core is a rewrite of the original ASP.NET framework, designed to be faster, more flexible, and more efficient. Here are a few reasons why ASP.NET Core is a great choice for back-end development:

- **Performance and Scalability:** ASP.NET Core is optimized for performance, making it one of the fastest web frameworks available. It has built-in features for caching, session management, and asynchronous programming, which are essential for building high-performance web applications that can handle a large number of concurrent users.
- **Cross-Platform Development:** ASP.NET Core is cross-platform, which means developers can build and deploy applications on various operating systems, including Windows, macOS, and Linux. This flexibility allows teams to use their preferred development environment while ensuring that their applications can run on different platforms.
- **Built-In Security Features:** Security is a top priority for any web application. ASP.NET Core provides several built-in security features, including support for HTTPS, authentication, and authorization. It also has strong integration with identity providers, making it easier to implement secure authentication mechanisms such as OAuth, OpenID Connect, and JWT.
- **MVC Architecture:** ASP.NET Core follows the Model-View-Controller (MVC) architecture, which helps developers separate concerns in their applications. The MVC pattern organizes code into distinct areas for data (Model), user interface (View), and business logic (Controller), making it easier to maintain and scale applications.
- **Dependency Injection:** ASP.NET Core has built-in support for dependency injection, a design pattern that improves code modularity, testability, and maintainability. By decoupling components from each other, dependency injection enables developers to build loosely coupled

systems, making their applications more flexible and easier to maintain.

Angular: A Dynamic Front-End Framework

Angular, developed and maintained by Google, is one of the most popular frameworks for building dynamic, single-page web applications (SPAs). Angular provides a powerful toolset for creating rich user interfaces and responsive web applications. Here's why Angular is a perfect complement to ASP.NET Core:

- **Component-Based Architecture:** Angular's component-based architecture promotes reusability and modularity. Developers can build self-contained components that encapsulate HTML, CSS, and JavaScript, making it easier to manage and scale large applications.
- **Two-Way Data Binding:** Angular's two-way data binding simplifies the synchronization between the model and the view. This means that any changes made to the user interface are immediately reflected in the application's data, and vice versa, reducing the amount of boilerplate code required to keep the UI and data in sync.
- **Dependency Injection:** Like ASP.NET Core, Angular also supports dependency injection, enabling the separation of concerns and improving the testability and maintainability of applications.
- **TypeScript:** Angular is built using TypeScript, a superset of JavaScript that adds static types to the language. TypeScript provides enhanced tooling, error checking, and code predictability, making it easier to develop large-scale applications with fewer bugs.
- **Routing and Navigation:** Angular's powerful routing module allows developers to manage navigation between views seamlessly. With features like lazy loading, Angular ensures that only the necessary components are loaded when needed, improving application performance.
- **State Management:** Angular's ecosystem includes tools like RxJS for handling asynchronous data streams and NgRx for managing application state, enabling developers to build complex, responsive, and performant

SPAs.

Why Combine ASP.NET Core and Angular?

While ASP.NET Core and Angular are each powerful frameworks on their own, combining them provides several advantages, especially when building modern web applications. Here's why this combination is a popular choice for full-stack developers:

- **Separation of Concerns:** By using ASP.NET Core for the back-end and Angular for the front-end, you can clearly separate concerns between the server and the client. This allows for cleaner, more maintainable code and simplifies the development process by enabling independent development and deployment of the front-end and back-end.
- **Scalability:** Both ASP.NET Core and Angular are designed to scale with your application. Whether you're building a small startup project or an enterprise-grade solution, this stack will grow with your needs, ensuring that performance remains optimal as your user base increases.
- **Rich Ecosystems:** ASP.NET Core and Angular have extensive ecosystems, offering a wealth of libraries, tools, and resources that can speed up development and add advanced functionality to your application. From authentication libraries to UI components, you'll have everything you need to build robust, feature-rich applications.
- **Cross-Platform Compatibility:** With ASP.NET Core being cross-platform and Angular being entirely client-side, your applications can run on any operating system and be deployed to various environments, including cloud platforms like Azure and AWS.

The combination of ASP.NET Core and Angular offers full-stack developers a powerful, flexible, and efficient way to build modern web applications that are scalable, secure, and performant.

The Evolution of Modern Web Development

Web development has come a long way since the early days of static HTML pages. Over the years, the complexity and functionality of web applications have grown exponentially, driven by advancements in both front-end and back-end technologies.

Early Days: Static Web Pages

In the early days of the internet, web pages were static, meaning they were composed entirely of HTML and CSS. There was little to no interactivity, and web applications were essentially collections of linked pages that served static content. Users had to manually navigate between pages, and there was no dynamic content or real-time data.

The Rise of Dynamic Web Pages

The introduction of server-side scripting languages like PHP, ASP, and Java in the late 1990s and early 2000s revolutionized web development by enabling the creation of dynamic web pages. These pages were generated on the fly based on user input or data from databases, allowing for more interactive and personalized user experiences.

Around the same time, the emergence of content management systems (CMS) like WordPress and Drupal further simplified the development of dynamic websites, allowing non-technical users to create and manage web content.

Web 2.0 and the Advent of Rich User Experiences

The early 2000s saw the rise of Web 2.0, a term used to describe the shift from static websites to interactive web applications. Web 2.0 emphasized user-generated content, social interaction, and rich media. Technologies like AJAX (Asynchronous JavaScript and XML) played a pivotal role in this evolution by enabling web applications to fetch data from servers in the background without reloading the entire page.

This shift paved the way for the development of more complex and interactive web applications, including social media platforms, online shopping experiences, and web-based software solutions.

The Emergence of Single-Page Applications (SPAs)

As web applications became more sophisticated, developers sought ways to improve performance and user experience. One of the most significant advancements in this regard was the introduction of Single-Page Applications (SPAs). SPAs are web applications that load a single HTML page and dynamically update the content as the user interacts with the application. This approach reduces the need for full-page reloads, resulting in faster and more seamless user experiences.

Frameworks like Angular, React, and Vue.js were developed to facilitate the creation of SPAs, providing developers with powerful tools for building rich, interactive user interfaces.

Modern Web Development: Microservices, APIs, and Cloud Computing

In recent years, modern web development has been shaped by several key trends, including the rise of microservices architecture, the proliferation of APIs, and the growing importance of cloud computing.

- **Microservices Architecture:** In contrast to traditional monolithic applications, which are built as a single unit, microservices architecture involves breaking down an application into small, independent services that can be developed, deployed, and scaled independently. This approach offers greater flexibility, scalability, and resilience.
- **APIs (Application Programming Interfaces):** APIs have become the backbone of modern web development, enabling communication

between different services and applications. RESTful APIs, in particular, have become the standard for building web services that can be consumed by different clients, including web browsers, mobile apps, and IoT devices.

- **Cloud Computing:** The shift to cloud computing has transformed how web applications are developed, deployed, and maintained. Cloud platforms like Amazon Web Services (AWS), Microsoft Azure, and Google Cloud offer scalable infrastructure and services that enable developers to build, deploy, and scale applications without managing physical servers.

These trends have led to a more modular and scalable approach to web development, where different components of an application can be developed, deployed, and scaled independently. The combination of ASP.NET Core and Angular is well-suited to this modern development landscape, offering a flexible and powerful solution for building scalable web applications.

How to Use This Book

This book is designed to be a comprehensive guide for both beginners and experienced developers who want to master full-stack development with ASP.NET Core and Angular. Whether you are new to web development or have experience with other technologies, this book will provide you with the knowledge and skills you need to build modern web applications from scratch.

Here's how to make the most of this book:

1. **Follow the Chapters Sequentially**: The book is structured in a way that allows you to build your knowledge progressively. Each chapter builds upon the concepts introduced in the previous ones. It's recommended to follow the chapters in order, especially if you're new to full-stack development.
2. **Hands-On Practice**: This book is packed with real-world examples,

code snippets, and projects. Make sure to follow along with the examples and practice the code on your own. The best way to learn full-stack development is through hands-on experience.

3. **Use the Provided Resources**: Throughout the book, you'll find references to additional resources, such as official documentation, tutorials, and community forums. These resources are invaluable for deepening your understanding and staying updated on the latest developments in ASP.NET Core and Angular.

4. **Customize the Projects**: The projects in this book are designed to give you practical experience, but don't be afraid to customize them to suit your needs. Experiment with different features, add new functionality, and challenge yourself to go beyond the examples provided.

5. **Keep Learning**: Web development is a constantly evolving field. Even after completing this book, continue learning by staying up to date with new versions of ASP.NET Core and Angular, exploring new tools and libraries, and working on real-world projects.

By the end of this book, you'll have a solid foundation in full-stack development with ASP.NET Core and Angular. You'll be equipped with the skills and knowledge to build dynamic, scalable, and high-performance web applications that can run on any platform.

Chapter 1: Getting Started with ASP.NET Core and Angular

I n this chapter, you will embark on your journey to become proficient in full-stack development by setting up the development environment for ASP.NET Core and Angular, two powerful technologies that, when combined, allow you to build scalable, efficient web applications. You will learn how to install the necessary tools and frameworks, and you will create your first API using ASP.NET Core, as well as your first Angular application.

By the end of this chapter, you will have a solid understanding of the tools required, how to structure your project, and how to set up a basic full-stack application. This will lay the foundation for more advanced topics in subsequent chapters.

Setting Up the Development Environment

Before we begin writing code, it's crucial to set up your development environment correctly. This ensures that everything works smoothly as you build your applications. For full-stack development with ASP.NET Core and Angular, you will need a few tools:

1. **Visual Studio or Visual Studio Code**
2. **.NET Core SDK**

3. **Node.js (for Angular)**
4. **Angular CLI (Command-Line Interface)**

Choosing Your Code Editor: Visual Studio vs. Visual Studio Code

When working with ASP.NET Core and Angular, having a suitable code editor is vital. Microsoft offers two popular editors: **Visual Studio** and **Visual Studio Code**.

Visual Studio

Visual Studio is an Integrated Development Environment (IDE) that provides a comprehensive set of tools for building web, desktop, mobile, and cloud applications. It has built-in support for ASP.NET Core and is an excellent choice if you're looking for a more robust environment with features such as:

- Powerful debugging tools
- Code navigation and refactoring
- Built-in Git integration
- Automated testing and deployment features

Visual Studio Community is a free version that is more than sufficient for most full-stack development projects.

Visual Studio Code

On the other hand, **Visual Studio Code (VS Code)** is a lightweight, cross-platform code editor. It is fast, highly customizable, and supports various programming languages. With the right extensions, Visual Studio Code is more than capable of handling both ASP.NET Core and Angular development.

VS Code is often preferred by developers who like more control over their development environment and appreciate its simplicity and flexibility. It also supports a wide range of extensions, including tools for .NET Core and Angular development.

For this book, we will use **Visual Studio Code** for its lightweight nature and broad community support. However, if you prefer Visual Studio, feel free to use it, as the steps will be quite similar.

Installing Visual Studio Code

1. Visit the Visual Studio Code website and download the installer for your operating system (Windows, macOS, or Linux).
2. Run the installer and follow the setup instructions.
3. Once installed, launch Visual Studio Code.

Now that you have your code editor installed, the next step is to install the **.NET Core SDK** and the **Angular CLI**.

Installing .NET Core SDK

The **.NET Core SDK** (Software Development Kit) provides the tools needed to build and run ASP.NET Core applications. It includes the .NET runtime, libraries, and command-line tools to develop and run your projects.

To install the .NET Core SDK:

1. Go to the .NET download page.
2. Choose the latest stable version of the **.NET SDK** for your platform (Windows, macOS, or Linux).
3. Download and install the SDK by following the instructions on the page.

After installation, verify that the SDK is installed correctly by opening a terminal (Command Prompt or PowerShell on Windows, or Terminal on macOS/Linux) and running the following command:

```bash
Copy code
```

```
dotnet --version
```

You should see the version number of the installed .NET Core SDK.

Installing ASP.NET Core Workload in Visual Studio Code

Next, you'll need to install the **C# extension** in Visual Studio Code to support ASP.NET Core development. Here's how to do that:

1. Open Visual Studio Code.
2. Go to the Extensions view by clicking the square icon on the sidebar or pressing Ctrl + Shift + X.
3. Search for "**C#**" in the Extensions Marketplace.
4. Install the extension by **Microsoft**, which provides support for .NET development, including debugging, IntelliSense, and more.

Once the extension is installed, Visual Studio Code is ready to handle .NET Core projects.

Installing Node.js

Angular requires **Node.js**, a runtime environment that allows you to execute JavaScript code outside of the browser. Node.js also comes with **npm** (Node Package Manager), which you'll use to install and manage Angular dependencies.

Steps to Install Node.js

1. Visit the Node.js download page.
2. Download the **LTS** (Long-Term Support) version, which is more stable for development projects.
3. Run the installer and follow the installation instructions.

After installation, verify the installation by running the following command in your terminal:

```bash
Copy code
node -v
npm -v
```

You should see the version numbers of both **Node.js** and **npm**.

Installing the Angular CLI

The **Angular CLI (Command Line Interface)** is a powerful tool that simplifies the process of creating and managing Angular projects. With the Angular CLI, you can generate components, services, routes, and much more with a single command, making development faster and easier.

To Install the Angular CLI:

Open your terminal and run the following command:

```bash
Copy code
npm install -g @angular/cli
```

This installs the Angular CLI globally on your machine. Once installed, verify the installation by running:

```bash
Copy code
ng version
```

This command will display the Angular CLI version along with other details about the installation.

Now that we have set up the development environment, it's time to dive into understanding the structure of ASP.NET Core and Angular projects.

Overview of ASP.NET Core and Angular Structure

ASP.NET Core Project Structure

When you create an ASP.NET Core project, it follows a specific structure that makes it easy to organize and manage your application. Let's take a look at the key components of an ASP.NET Core project:

- **Controllers**: Controllers are responsible for handling incoming HTTP requests and returning responses. In ASP.NET Core, you typically create controllers to manage different parts of your application, such as users, products, or orders. Each controller contains methods (known as "actions") that map to specific routes in your application.
- **Models**: Models represent the data and business logic of your application. They are often used to interact with the database and contain validation rules, data relationships, and more.
- **Views**: Although we won't be using views much in a typical API project, they are part of ASP.NET Core's MVC architecture. Views are responsible for rendering the user interface in traditional web applications. However, since Angular will handle the front-end in this case, views are not the focus here.
- **Startup.cs**: The **Startup.cs** file configures services and the app's middleware pipeline. It plays a crucial role in setting up features like authentication, routing, and error handling. This file is central to the ASP.NET Core application lifecycle.
- **Program.cs**: This file contains the main entry point of your application. It is responsible for configuring the web server and bootstrapping the application.
- **appsettings.json**: This file is used to store application settings such as connection strings, logging configurations, and other environment-

specific configurations.

Angular Project Structure

Angular projects follow a modular architecture that allows you to break down your application into small, reusable components. Let's look at the key components of an Angular project:

- **src/app**: This is where your application's source code resides. Inside this folder, you will find your main app component (app.component.ts), along with other components, services, and modules.
- **Components**: Components are the building blocks of an Angular application. They consist of three main files:
- component.ts (TypeScript file): Contains the logic and data binding for the component.
- component.html: Defines the template (view) for the component, which controls how the UI looks.
- component.css: Contains the styles specific to the component.
- **Services**: Services in Angular are used to handle business logic, data retrieval, and communication with the back-end (such as an API). Services can be injected into components to keep your application modular and maintainable.
- **Modules**: Angular applications are divided into **modules**, with the main one being app.module.ts. Each module groups together components, services, and other modules, allowing you to organize your app into functional sections.
- **Routing**: Angular's routing module manages navigation between different views or components in your application. It allows users to switch between different "pages" without reloading the whole application.

Now that you understand the basic structure of both ASP.NET Core and Angular, it's time to create your first application and API.

Creating Your First API and Angular Application

Step 1: Creating an ASP.NET Core Web API

To create a new ASP.NET Core Web API project, follow these steps:

1. **Open Visual Studio Code** or Visual Studio.
2. Open the integrated terminal by selecting **View > Terminal**.
3. Navigate to the folder where you want to create your project, and run the following command:

```bash
Copy code
dotnet new webapi -n MyFirstApi
```

This command creates a new ASP.NET Core Web API project named **MyFirstApi**.

1. After the project is created, navigate into the project folder:

```bash
Copy code
cd MyFirstApi
```

1. Open the project in Visual Studio Code:

```bash
Copy code
```

code .

Your project will contain several files, including Controllers, Models, and the Startup.cs file. Let's modify the default controller to return some data.

Modifying the Default Controller

1. Open the **Controllers** folder and find the WeatherForecastController. cs file.
2. Replace the default code with the following:

```csharp
Copy code
using Microsoft.AspNetCore.Mvc;
using System.Collections.Generic;

namespace MyFirstApi.Controllers
{
    [ApiController]
    [Route("api/[controller]")]
    public class HelloWorldController : ControllerBase
    {
        [HttpGet]
        public IEnumerable<string> Get()
        {
            return new string[] { "Hello", "World" };
        }
    }
}
```

This code creates a simple API that returns an array with the words "Hello" and "World."

1. Run the application using the following command:

```bash
Copy code
dotnet run
```

Open a browser and navigate to https://localhost:5001/api/helloworld. You should see the response:

```json
Copy code
["Hello", "World"]
```

Congratulations! You've just created your first ASP.NET Core Web API.

Step 2: Creating an Angular Application

Now, let's create the front-end using Angular.

1. Open the terminal and run the following command to create a new Angular project:

```bash
Copy code
ng new my-angular-app
```

1. You will be prompted with a few options:

- **Would you like to add Angular routing?** Yes
- **Which stylesheet format would you like to use?** Choose your preferred format (CSS, SCSS, etc.).

1. Once the project is created, navigate into the project folder:

```bash
bash
Copy code
cd my-angular-app
```

1. Open the project in Visual Studio Code:

```bash
bash
Copy code
code .
```

1. Run the Angular application by using the following command:

```bash
bash
Copy code
ng serve
```

1. Open your browser and navigate to http://localhost:4200. You should see the default Angular welcome page.

Step 3: Consuming the API in Angular

Now that we have both the ASP.NET Core Web API and the Angular application running, let's consume the API in Angular.

1. Open the app.component.ts file in your Angular project.
2. Import the HttpClient module and inject it into the constructor:

```typescript
Copy code
import { Component } from '@angular/core';
import { HttpClient } from '@angular/common/http';

@Component({
  selector: 'app-root',
  templateUrl: './app.component.html',
  styleUrls: ['./app.component.css']
})
export class AppComponent {
  title = 'my-angular-app';
  helloWorldData: string[];

  constructor(private http: HttpClient) {
    this.http.get<string[]>('https://localhost:5001/api/helloworld')
      .subscribe(data => {
        this.helloWorldData = data;
      });
  }
}
```

1. Open the app.component.html file and display the data:

```html
Copy code
<div>
  <h1>ASP.NET Core and Angular Integration</h1>
  <ul>
    <li *ngFor="let word of helloWorldData">{{ word }}</li>
  </ul>
</div>
```

1. Finally, run the Angular application again with:

```bash
bash
Copy code
ng serve
```

Now, if you open http://localhost:4200, you should see the data fetched from your ASP.NET Core API being displayed on the Angular front-end.

Conclusion

In this chapter, we laid the groundwork for full-stack development with ASP.NET Core and Angular. You've set up your development environment, learned the basic structure of both frameworks, and created a simple API and Angular application.

Chapter 2: Building a RESTful Web API with ASP.NET Core

B uilding a powerful and scalable back-end is an essential aspect of any full-stack development project. In this chapter, we will focus on creating a **RESTful Web API** using **ASP.NET Core**. You will gain a thorough understanding of RESTful principles, learn how to create controllers and endpoints, work with models and Data Transfer Objects (DTOs), and implement **Dependency Injection** in your API. By the end of this chapter, you'll be well-equipped to create scalable and maintainable APIs for modern web applications.

Understanding RESTful Principles

Before diving into building your API, it's important to understand the principles that guide the development of **RESTful APIs**. REST (Representational State Transfer) is an architectural style that defines a set of constraints and principles for building scalable and efficient web services.

Here are the key RESTful principles:

1. Statelessness

A RESTful service is stateless, meaning each request from a client to a server must contain all the information necessary to understand and process the request. The server does not store any client-specific information between requests. This ensures that each interaction is independent, which simplifies the application architecture and improves scalability.

2. Client-Server Architecture

In a RESTful system, the client and server are decoupled. The client is responsible for the user interface and experience, while the server handles the data processing and business logic. This separation of concerns makes both sides of the application more flexible and maintainable.

3. Uniform Interface

The uniform interface is a central concept in REST. It simplifies the architecture and enables developers to interact with the API in a consistent manner. This is typically achieved using standard HTTP methods like:

- **GET**: Retrieve resources.
- **POST**: Create new resources.
- **PUT**: Update existing resources.
- **DELETE**: Delete resources.

Additionally, URIs (Uniform Resource Identifiers) are used to identify resources, and the data is often exchanged in JSON format.

4. Resource-Based URLs

In a RESTful API, resources (such as users, products, and orders) are the main entities that the client interacts with. Resources are identified by **URLs** (Uniform Resource Locators), which follow a standard structure. For example, a resource for fetching a list of products may look like this:

```bash
Copy code
GET /api/products
```

The URL structure is intuitive and consistent, making it easier to navigate and understand the API.

5. Representation of Resources

Resources are represented in different formats, commonly JSON or XML. The client specifies the desired format in the request headers (using the Accept header), and the server responds accordingly. This flexibility allows APIs to work with a variety of clients, such as web browsers, mobile apps, and other services.

6. Stateless Communication and Cacheability

Each response from the server must clearly indicate whether the data is cacheable. Cacheable responses improve the efficiency of interactions, especially in scenarios where the same data is requested multiple times.

7. Layered System

A RESTful API can be structured in layers, allowing developers to implement additional layers such as load balancers, proxies, and gateways. This layered architecture enhances the scalability, security, and manageability of the system.

8. Hypermedia as the Engine of Application State (HATEOAS)

One of the more advanced principles of REST is **HATEOAS**. In this principle, responses from the API include not only the requested data but also additional information on what other actions the client can perform (e.g., links to other related resources). HATEOAS improves navigation in APIs by making them more discoverable.

Creating Controllers and Endpoints

In ASP.NET Core, **controllers** are classes that handle incoming HTTP requests, process them, and return responses. Each method in a controller corresponds to an **endpoint**, which can be accessed via a specific URL and HTTP method.

Step 1: Creating a New Controller

In this section, we will create a basic controller to handle operations for a simple **Product** resource. Let's begin by creating a new controller.

1. Open your project in **Visual Studio Code**.
2. Navigate to the **Controllers** folder.
3. Right-click on the **Controllers** folder and select **New File**. Name it ProductsController.cs.
4. Inside the ProductsController.cs file, create a new controller class:

```csharp
Copy code
using Microsoft.AspNetCore.Mvc;
using System.Collections.Generic;
```

```
namespace MyFirstApi.Controllers
{
    [Route("api/[controller]")]
    [ApiController]
    public class ProductsController : ControllerBase
    {
        [HttpGet]
        public ActionResult<IEnumerable<string>> Get()
        {
            return new string[] { "Product1", "Product2",
            "Product3" };
        }
    }
}
```

Explanation of the Code

- **[ApiController]**: This attribute indicates that the controller is an API controller, which simplifies model binding, validation, and response formatting.
- **[Route("api/[controller]")]**: This specifies the route for the controller. The placeholder [controller] is replaced by the controller's name (Products), resulting in the following URL for accessing the controller: api/products.
- **[HttpGet]**: This attribute maps HTTP GET requests to the Get() method, which returns a list of products.

The ProductsController we just created can now handle GET requests to https://localhost:5001/api/products and return a list of strings.

Step 2: Testing the API Endpoint

To test this endpoint:

1. Run the application using the following command:

```bash
Copy code
dotnet run
```

1. Open your browser and navigate to https://localhost:5001/api/produc ts. You should see the following JSON response:

```json
Copy code
["Product1", "Product2", "Product3"]
```

Congratulations! You've successfully created your first API controller and endpoint in ASP.NET Core.

Working with Models and Data Transfer Objects (DTOs)

Understanding Models in ASP.NET Core

In most applications, you will need to work with **models**, which represent the data structure or the entities of your application. Models are used to define how data is stored and manipulated.

For example, let's define a **Product** model that contains the properties of a product.

1. In the root of your project, create a folder called **Models**.
2. Inside the **Models** folder, create a file named Product.cs.
3. Define the **Product** class as follows:

```csharp
Copy code
namespace MyFirstApi.Models
{
    public class Product
    {
        public int Id { get; set; }
        public string Name { get; set; }
        public decimal Price { get; set; }
        public string Description { get; set; }
    }
}
```

This class defines a simple product with four properties: Id, Name, Price, and Description.

Data Transfer Objects (DTOs)

In ASP.NET Core, it is common to use **Data Transfer Objects (DTOs)** to encapsulate the data sent between the client and the server. DTOs are often simpler versions of models and are used to reduce the amount of data sent over the network.

For instance, you may want to create a **ProductDTO** that only contains the essential fields that should be exposed to the client.

1. In the **Models** folder, create a file named ProductDTO.cs.
2. Define the **ProductDTO** class as follows:

```csharp
Copy code
namespace MyFirstApi.Models
{
    public class ProductDTO
    {
        public int Id { get; set; }
        public string Name { get; set; }
        public decimal Price { get; set; }
    }
}
```

In this case, the **ProductDTO** only contains the Id, Name, and Price properties, excluding sensitive or unnecessary fields like Description.

Creating a Repository for Products

In a real-world application, you will most likely need to interact with a database to fetch, create, update, and delete data. To keep the application organized and scalable, we'll implement a **Repository Pattern**.

The Repository Pattern abstracts the logic for interacting with data sources. Let's create a simple repository for handling product operations.

1. In the root of your project, create a folder called **Repositories**.
2. Inside the **Repositories** folder, create an interface named IProductRepository.cs.
3. Define the IProductRepository interface:

```csharp
Copy code
using System.Collections.Generic;
using MyFirstApi.Models;

namespace MyFirstApi.Repositories
```

```csharp
{
    public interface IProductRepository
    {
        IEnumerable<Product> GetAllProducts();
        Product GetProductById(int id);
        void AddProduct(Product product);
        void UpdateProduct(Product product);
        void DeleteProduct(int id);
    }
}
```

This interface defines the operations we can perform on the product data, such as retrieving all products, retrieving a product by ID, adding a new product, updating an existing product, and deleting a product.

1. Next, create the repository implementation. In the **Repositories** folder, create a file named ProductRepository.cs.
2. Define the ProductRepository class:

```csharp
csharp
Copy code
using System.Collections.Generic;
using System.Linq;
using MyFirstApi.Models;

namespace MyFirstApi.Repositories
{
    public class ProductRepository : IProductRepository
    {
        private List<Product> _products = new List<Product>
        {
            new Product { Id = 1, Name = "Product1", Price =
            19.99M, Description = "Descripti
```

Chapter 3: Introduction to Angular Framework

Angular is a powerful, versatile front-end framework for building dynamic, single-page applications (SPAs). It has gained immense popularity due to its component-based architecture, efficient data binding, and comprehensive tooling that enables developers to create robust and maintainable web applications.

In this chapter, you'll learn about Angular's core architecture, including components, modules, services, and routing. We will explore the power of the Angular CLI, which simplifies many development tasks, and finally, we will delve into Angular's routing and navigation to build scalable and dynamic SPAs.

The Angular Component-Based Architecture

Understanding Components

In Angular, components are the fundamental building blocks of the application. A component is a class that controls a portion of the user interface, often referred to as a "view." Each component consists of three key parts:

1. **HTML template**: Defines the UI layout and structure.

2. **TypeScript class**: Contains the logic and data-binding functions for the template.
3. **CSS or SCSS**: Styles the template.

Angular applications are built by composing multiple components, making it easier to divide the app into reusable, self-contained pieces. This modular approach promotes better organization, maintainability, and scalability.

Structure of a Component

Each Angular component typically has the following files:

- **component.ts**: The TypeScript file, which contains the class definition, handles events, and manages data binding.
- **component.html**: The HTML file that contains the view or template.
- **component.css (or .scss)**: This file contains styles specific to the component, ensuring that each component can be styled independently.

Example of a Basic Component

Let's create a simple component that displays a message.

```typescript
Copy code
// src/app/hello-world/hello-world.component.ts
import { Component } from '@angular/core';

@Component({
  selector: 'app-hello-world',
  templateUrl: './hello-world.component.html',
  styleUrls: ['./hello-world.component.css']
})
export class HelloWorldComponent {
  message = 'Hello, Angular!';
}
```

```
html
Copy code
<!-- src/app/hello-world/hello-world.component.html -->
<div>
  <h1>{{ message }}</h1>
</div>
```

In the example above:

- The **selector** is used to identify this component in the HTML. You can place <app-hello-world></app-hello-world> anywhere in the application to display this component.
- The **templateUrl** links to the HTML file that defines the view.
- The **styleUrls** property links to the CSS file that styles the component.

Data Binding in Angular

One of the most powerful features of Angular is its **data binding** capability. Data binding allows you to easily synchronize data between the UI and the component's logic.

There are four types of data binding in Angular:

1. **Interpolation (One-Way Data Binding)**: Allows you to display data from the component in the template using {{ }} syntax.

```
html
Copy code
<h1>{{ message }}</h1>
```

1. **Property Binding**: Binds a property in the component to a property of an HTML element.

```html
html
Copy code
<input [value]="message" />
```

1. **Event Binding**: Binds an event (like click) from the template to a function in the component.

```html
html
Copy code
<button (click)="sayHello()">Click Me</button>
```

1. **Two-Way Binding**: Combines property and event binding to synchronize data in both directions (from the component to the template and vice versa). This is commonly used with forms.

```html
html
Copy code
<input [(ngModel)]="message" />
```

Component Communication

In a real-world application, you will often need to have components communicate with each other. Angular facilitates communication between parent and child components using **Input** and **Output** decorators.

- **@Input()**: Allows the parent component to pass data to a child component.

- **@Output()**: Allows the child component to emit events to the parent.

Here's an example of how parent-child communication works:

```typescript
Copy code
// child.component.ts
import { Component, Input } from '@angular/core';

@Component({
  selector: 'app-child',
  template: `<p>Child message: {{ message }}</p>`
})
export class ChildComponent {
  @Input() message: string;
}
```

```html
Copy code
<!-- parent.component.html -->
<app-child [message]="parentMessage"></app-child>
```

This simple example shows how data flows from the parent component (parentMessage) to the child component (message).

Creating Angular Components, Modules, and Services

Creating Components with Angular CLI

One of the most efficient ways to generate Angular components is by using the **Angular CLI** (Command Line Interface). With a single command, you can scaffold a new component, and Angular CLI will automatically create the necessary files and configurations for you.

To generate a component using Angular CLI, open a terminal and run the following command:

```bash
Copy code
ng generate component my-new-component
```

This command creates the following files in the **src/app/my-new-component/** directory:

- my-new-component.component.ts: The TypeScript class file.
- my-new-component.component.html: The template file.
- my-new-component.component.css: The styles file.
- my-new-component.component.spec.ts: The unit test file for the component.

Angular CLI also automatically declares the new component in the module's declarations array, which means it is ready to be used in your application.

Understanding Angular Modules

In Angular, an application is divided into **modules**. Modules help organize the application by grouping related components, services, and other functionality into a cohesive unit. Every Angular application has at least one module, called the **root module** (typically AppModule).

Each module can:

- Declare which components it contains.
- Import other modules (such as forms or HTTP modules).
- Provide services that can be injected throughout the module.

Here's a basic example of an **Angular module**:

```typescript
Copy code
```

```
// src/app/app.module.ts
import { BrowserModule } from '@angular/platform-browser';
import { NgModule } from '@angular/core';
import { AppComponent } from './app.component';
import { HelloWorldComponent } from
'./hello-world/hello-world.component';

@NgModule({
  declarations: [
    AppComponent,
    HelloWorldComponent
  ],
  imports: [
    BrowserModule
  ],
  providers: [],
  bootstrap: [AppComponent]
})
export class AppModule { }
```

In this example, AppModule declares two components: AppComponent and HelloWorldComponent. The BrowserModule is imported because it is necessary to run the app in a browser.

Creating Services for Business Logic

In Angular, **services** are used to encapsulate business logic and handle external communication, such as retrieving data from an API or managing application state. Services are typically injected into components and other services using Angular's **Dependency Injection** system.

To create a service using the Angular CLI, run the following command:

```
bash
Copy code
ng generate service my-new-service
```

This command generates a TypeScript file for the service:

```typescript
Copy code
// src/app/my-new-service.service.ts
import { Injectable } from '@angular/core';

@Injectable({
  providedIn: 'root'
})
export class MyNewService {
  constructor() { }

  getMessage() {
    return 'Service says hello!';
  }
}
```

By adding the @Injectable decorator with the providedIn property set to 'root', Angular makes this service available to the entire application without needing to manually add it to the providers array in a module.

Using Services in a Component

Now, let's see how to inject and use this service in a component.

1. Open the **hello-world.component.ts** file.
2. Inject the MyNewService into the component:

```typescript
Copy code
import { Component } from '@angular/core';
import { MyNewService } from '../my-new-service.service';

@Component({
```

```
  selector: 'app-hello-world',
  templateUrl: './hello-world.component.html',
  styleUrls: ['./hello-world.component.css']
})
export class HelloWorldComponent {
  message: string;

  constructor(private myNewService: MyNewService) {
    this.message = myNewService.getMessage();
  }
}
```

In this example, the **MyNewService** is injected into the HelloWorldCom
ponent's constructor, and the getMessage() method is called to retrieve a
message.

Angular CLI: A Powerful Tool for Development

The **Angular CLI** is an indispensable tool for Angular development. It
simplifies common development tasks such as project creation, code
generation, testing, and deployment. Let's explore some of the most useful
commands provided by Angular CLI.

Creating a New Angular Project

The first and most important command you will use is ng new, which creates
a new Angular project.

```bash
Copy code
ng new my-angular-app
```

This command will prompt you with several options:

- **Would you like to add Angular routing?**: Select Yes if you want to include routing in your project.

- **Which stylesheet format would you like to use?**: Choose between CSS, SCSS, or other options.

After you answer these prompts, the CLI will generate a new Angular project with all the necessary configurations.

Serving the Application

Once the project is created, you can serve the application using the ng serve command. This starts a development server and opens the application in your browser.

```bash
Copy code
ng serve
```

The application is available at http://localhost:4200 by default.

Generating Components, Services, and Modules

Angular CLI provides commands for generating new components, services, and modules:

- **Generate Component**: Creates a new Angular component.

```bash
Copy code
ng generate component my-component
```

- **Generate Service**: Creates a new service.

```bash
Copy code
ng generate service my-service
```

- **Generate Module**: Creates a new module.

```bash
Copy code
ng generate module my-module
```

Running Tests

Angular CLI includes built-in support for running unit and end-to-end tests. To run unit tests, use the following command:

```bash
Copy code
ng test
```

This command runs the unit tests and opens a browser where the results are displayed.

For end-to-end testing, you can use the ng e2e command:

```bash
Copy code
ng e2e
```

This command runs end-to-end tests using Protractor.

Introduction to Angular Routing and Navigation

In any web application, routing plays a crucial role in navigating between different views. Angular's powerful routing module allows developers to define routes, navigate between views, and even implement features like lazy loading for optimizing performance.

Basic Routing Setup

To set up routing in an Angular application, you need to define routes and associate them with components.

1. Open the app-routing.module.ts file. This file is automatically created when you select "Yes" for Angular routing during project setup.
2. Define your routes as follows:

```typescript
Copy code
import { NgModule } from '@angular/core';
import { RouterModule, Routes } from '@angular/router';
import { HelloWorldComponent } from
'./hello-world/hello-world.component';

const routes: Routes = [
  { path: 'hello', component: HelloWorldComponent },
  { path: '', redirectTo: '/hello', pathMatch: 'full' }
];

@NgModule({
  imports: [RouterModule.forRoot(routes)],
  exports: [RouterModule]
})
export class AppRoutingModule { }
```

In this example:

- The route 'hello' maps to the HelloWorldComponent.
- The default route (") redirects to the /hello path.

Adding Router Links

To navigate between routes, you can use Angular's **routerLink** directive.
Let's add a link to navigate to the HelloWorldComponent.

```html
Copy code
<nav>
  <a routerLink="/hello">Go to Hello World</a>
</nav>

<router-outlet></router-outlet>
```

The **routerLink** directive tells Angular to navigate to the /hello route when
the link is clicked. The **<router-outlet>** directive is where the component
associated with the route will be rendered.

Lazy Loading for Performance Optimization

Lazy loading is an optimization technique where Angular only loads a feature
module when it's needed. This improves performance by reducing the initial
load time of the application.

To implement lazy loading, you need to modify the routing configuration.

1. Create a new module for lazy loading:

```bash
Copy code
ng generate module lazy --route lazy --module app.module
```

This command creates a new module and configures it to be lazy-loaded when the /lazy route is accessed.

1. Update the app-routing.module.ts file:

```typescript
Copy code
const routes: Routes = [
  { path: 'lazy', loadChildren: () =>
  import('./lazy/lazy.module').then(m => m.LazyModule) }
];
```

Now, the LazyModule will only be loaded when the user navigates to the /lazy route, improving the application's performance.

Conclusion

In this chapter, you've gained a solid understanding of the core concepts of Angular's component-based architecture. You learned how to create components, modules, and services, and you explored the Angular CLI's powerful features to streamline development tasks. You also dived into Angular's routing system, which allows you to build dynamic, single-page applications with ease.

Chapter 4: Integrating ASP.NET Core Web API with Angular

I ntegrating the back-end and front-end of an application is a crucial step in full-stack development. In this chapter, we will focus on how to effectively connect your Angular application to the ASP.NET Core Web API you built in the previous chapters. We will explore the use of Angular's HTTPClient for consuming APIs, handling JSON data, configuring Cross-Origin Resource Sharing (CORS), and implementing error handling and validation in API requests.

By the end of this chapter, you will have a clear understanding of how to create a seamless connection between your Angular front end and ASP.NET Core back end, enabling you to build dynamic and interactive web applications.

Consuming APIs in Angular Using HTTPClient

Introduction to HTTPClient

The HTTPClient module in Angular is a powerful service that allows you to make HTTP requests to RESTful APIs. It provides an easy-to-use interface for sending and receiving data over HTTP, enabling you to interact with your back-end services.

46

To get started, you need to import the HttpClientModule in your Angular application. Here's how you can do that:

1. Open the app.module.ts file.
2. Import HttpClientModule from @angular/common/http.

```typescript
Copy code
import { NgModule } from '@angular/core';
import { BrowserModule } from '@angular/platform-browser';
import { HttpClientModule } from '@angular/common/http';
import { AppComponent } from './app.component';
import { AppRoutingModule } from './app-routing.module';

@NgModule({
  declarations: [
    AppComponent
  ],
  imports: [
    BrowserModule,
    AppRoutingModule,
    HttpClientModule // Importing HttpClientModule
  ],
  providers: [],
  bootstrap: [AppComponent]
})
export class AppModule { }
```

Making GET Requests

Now that you have imported the HttpClientModule, let's create a service to consume the API and retrieve product data.

1. Generate a new service using Angular CLI:

```bash
bash
Copy code
ng generate service product
```

1. Open the newly created product.service.ts file and import HttpClient:

```typescript
typescript
Copy code
import { Injectable } from '@angular/core';
import { HttpClient } from '@angular/common/http';
import { Observable } from 'rxjs';
import { Product } from './models/product.model';

@Injectable({
  providedIn: 'root'
})
export class ProductService {
  private apiUrl = 'https://localhost:5001/api/products';

  constructor(private http: HttpClient) { }

  getProducts(): Observable<Product[]> {
    return this.http.get<Product[]>(this.apiUrl);
  }
}
```

Explanation of the Code

- **HttpClient**: The service is injected with HttpClient, allowing it to make HTTP requests.
- **apiUrl**: This is the URL of the ASP.NET Core Web API endpoint that provides product data.
- **getProducts()**: This method makes a GET request to the API and returns

an Observable of the product list.

Using the Product Service in a Component

To display the product data in a component, we'll modify the hello-world.component.ts file to use the ProductService.

1. Inject the ProductService in the HelloWorldComponent:

```typescript
Copy code
import { Component, OnInit } from '@angular/core';
import { ProductService } from '../product.service';
import { Product } from '../models/product.model';

@Component({
  selector: 'app-hello-world',
  templateUrl: './hello-world.component.html',
  styleUrls: ['./hello-world.component.css']
})
export class HelloWorldComponent implements OnInit {
  products: Product[];

  constructor(private productService: ProductService) { }

  ngOnInit(): void {
    this.productService.getProducts().subscribe(data => {
      this.products = data;
    });
  }
}
```

Template for Displaying Products

Next, update the hello-world.component.html file to display the products:

```html
html
Copy code
<div>
  <h1>Products</h1>
  <ul>
    <li *ngFor="let product of products">
      {{ product.name }} - ${{ product.price }}
    </li>
  </ul>
</div>
```

Making POST Requests

In addition to GET requests, you will also need to implement POST requests to add new products to your API.

1. Update the ProductService to include a method for adding a product:

```typescript
typescript
Copy code
addProduct(product: Product): Observable<Product> {
  return this.http.post<Product>(this.apiUrl, product);
}
```

Using the POST Method in a Component

To test the POST functionality, create a form in your component to submit new product data.

1. Update the hello-world.component.html file to include a form:

```html
Copy code
<form (ngSubmit)="onSubmit()">
  <input type="text" [(ngModel)]="newProduct.name" name="name"
  placeholder="Product Name" required>
  <input type="number" [(ngModel)]="newProduct.price"
  name="price" placeholder="Product Price" required>
  <button type="submit">Add Product</button>
</form>
```

1. In the hello-world.component.ts, add the logic to handle form submission:

```typescript
Copy code
newProduct: Product = { id: 0, name: '', price: 0 };

onSubmit(): void {
  this.productService.addProduct(this.newProduct).subscribe(product
  => {
    this.products.push(product);
    this.newProduct = { id: 0, name: '', price: 0 }; // Reset the
    form
  });
}
```

This implementation allows you to add new products to the API and update the list displayed in the component.

Handling JSON Data and API Responses

Working with JSON Data

When dealing with APIs, JSON (JavaScript Object Notation) is the most common format for sending and receiving data. Angular's HTTPClient automatically handles the serialization and deserialization of JSON data, allowing you to work with TypeScript objects seamlessly.

Receiving JSON Responses

In our earlier example, when we called this.http.get<Product[]>(this.api Url), Angular automatically parsed the JSON response from the API into a TypeScript array of Product objects. The response structure is directly mapped to the Product model, which we defined earlier.

Error Handling with HTTPClient

It's essential to handle errors that may occur during API calls to provide a better user experience and debug effectively. Angular allows you to manage errors using the catchError operator from the rxjs/operators library.

Here's how to implement error handling in the ProductService:

1. Import catchError and throwError from rxjs:

```typescript
Copy code
import { catchError } from 'rxjs/operators';
import { throwError } from 'rxjs';
```

1. Update the getProducts method to include error handling:

```typescript
Copy code
getProducts(): Observable<Product[]> {
  return this.http.get<Product[]>(this.apiUrl).pipe(
    catchError(this.handleError)
  );
}

private handleError(error: any): Observable<never> {
  console.error('An error occurred:', error); // Log the error to
  the console
  return throwError('Something went wrong; please try again
  later.');
}
```

Displaying Error Messages in the Component

To provide feedback to the user, you can display error messages in the component when an API call fails. Update the HelloWorldComponent as follows:

1. Add an error message variable:

```typescript
Copy code
errorMessage: string = '';
```

1. Update the ngOnInit method to set the error message if an error occurs:

```typescript
Copy code
ngOnInit(): void {
  this.productService.getProducts().subscribe(
    data => {
      this.products = data;
      this.errorMessage = ''; // Clear error message on
      successful response
    },
    error => {
      this.errorMessage = error; // Set the error message
    }
  );
}
```

1. Update the template to display the error message:

```html
Copy code
<div *ngIf="errorMessage" class="error">{{ errorMessage }}</div>
```

Handling HTTP Errors Globally

For larger applications, you may want to handle HTTP errors globally. This can be done using an HttpInterceptor. An interceptor allows you to intercept HTTP requests and responses globally and is useful for logging errors or adding authentication tokens.

1. Create an interceptor:

```bash
bash
Copy code
ng generate interceptor httpError
```

1. Update the generated http-error.interceptor.ts file:

```typescript
typescript
Copy code
import { Injectable } from '@angular/core';
import { HttpEvent, HttpInterceptor, HttpHandler, HttpRequest,
HttpErrorResponse } from '@angular/common/http';
import { Observable, throwError } from 'rxjs';
import { catchError } from 'rxjs/operators';

@Injectable()
export class HttpErrorInterceptor implements HttpInterceptor {
  intercept(req: HttpRequest<any>, next: HttpHandler):
  Observable<HttpEvent<any>> {
    return next.handle(req).pipe(
      catchError((error: HttpErrorResponse) => {
        // Handle error globally
        console.error('HTTP Error:', error);
        return throwError(error);
      })
    );
  }
}
```

1. Register the interceptor in app.module.ts:

```typescript
typescript
Copy code
```

```
import { HTTP_INTERCEPTORS } from '@angular/common/http';
import { HttpErrorInterceptor } from './http-error.interceptor';

@NgModule({
  providers: [
    { provide: HTTP_INTERCEPTORS, useClass: HttpErrorInterceptor,
    multi: true }
  ]
})
```

This interceptor will log all HTTP errors that occur in the application and can be further enhanced to display user-friendly messages.

Cross-Origin Resource Sharing (CORS) Configuration

What is CORS?

CORS (Cross-Origin Resource Sharing) is a security feature implemented in web browsers that prevents JavaScript code running on one domain from making requests to another domain unless explicitly allowed. This is important when your Angular application is hosted on a different domain (or port) than your ASP.NET Core Web API.

Configuring CORS in ASP.NET Core

To enable CORS in your ASP.NET Core application, follow these steps:

1. Open the Startup.cs file.
2. In the ConfigureServices method, add the CORS services:

```
csharp
Copy code
```

```csharp
public void ConfigureServices(IServiceCollection services)
{
    services.AddCors(options =>
    {
        options.AddPolicy("AllowAllOrigins",
            builder =>
            {
                builder.AllowAnyOrigin()
                       .AllowAnyMethod()
                       .AllowAnyHeader();
            });
    });
    services.AddControllers();
}
```

In this example, we define a CORS policy named **AllowAllOrigins**, which allows any origin, method, and header. This is suitable for development but should be limited in production to specific origins.

1. In the Configure method, enable the CORS policy:

```csharp
csharp
Copy code
public void Configure(IApplicationBuilder app,
IWebHostEnvironment env)
{
    if (env.IsDevelopment())
    {
        app.UseDeveloperExceptionPage();
    }

    app.UseHttpsRedirection();

    app.UseRouting();

    app.UseCors("AllowAllOrigins"); // Enable CORS
```

```
    app.UseAuthorization();

    app.UseEndpoints(endpoints =>
    {
        endpoints.MapControllers();
    });
}
```

Testing CORS with Angular

Now that you've configured CORS in your ASP.NET Core API, you can test your Angular application to see if it successfully communicates with the API. Run your ASP.NET Core API and Angular application simultaneously and make sure that you can retrieve and manipulate data without any CORS-related errors in the console.

If everything is set up correctly, your Angular application should be able to communicate with the API without issues.

Error Handling and Validation in API Requests

Validation in ASP.NET Core API

Validating input data is crucial for maintaining data integrity and ensuring that the API behaves as expected. ASP.NET Core provides built-in data validation capabilities using **Data Annotations**.

1. Update the Product model to include validation attributes:

```
csharp
Copy code
```

58

```
using System.ComponentModel.DataAnnotations;

public class Product
{
    public int Id { get; set; }

    [Required(ErrorMessage = "Name is required.")]
    [StringLength(100, ErrorMessage = "Name cannot exceed 100
    characters.")]
    public string Name { get; set; }

    [Range(0.01, double.MaxValue, ErrorMessage = "Price must be
    greater than 0.")]
    public decimal Price { get; set; }

    public string Description { get; set; }
}
```

In this example:

- The **[Required]** attribute ensures that the Name property is not empty.
- The **[StringLength]** attribute limits the length of the Name.
- The **[Range]** attribute validates that the Price is greater than 0.

Handling Validation Errors in the API

When validation fails, ASP.NET Core will return a **400 Bad Request** response with a detailed error message. You can customize this behavior in your controller methods:

```csharp
Copy code
[HttpPost]
public ActionResult<Product> AddProduct(Product product)
{
    if (!ModelState.IsValid)
```

```
    {
        return BadRequest(ModelState); // Return validation errors
    }

    // Add product to the database (mocked here)
    return CreatedAtAction(nameof(GetProductById), new { id =
    product.Id }, product);
}
```

Client-Side Validation in Angular

To enhance user experience, you can implement client-side validation in your Angular application. This provides immediate feedback to users when they enter invalid data in forms.

1. Update the form in hello-world.component.html to include validation feedback:

```html
Copy code
<form (ngSubmit)="onSubmit()" #productForm="ngForm">
  <input type="text" [(ngModel)]="newProduct.name" name="name"
  placeholder="Product Name" required>
  <div *ngIf="productForm.controls.name?.invalid &&
  productForm.controls.name?.touched">
    <small class="error">Product Name is required.</small>
  </div>

  <input type="number" [(ngModel)]="newProduct.price"
  name="price" placeholder="Product Price" required>
  <div *ngIf="productForm.controls.price?.invalid &&
  productForm.controls.price?.touched">
    <small class="error">Price must be greater than 0.</small>
  </div>
```

```
<button type="submit" [disabled]="productForm.invalid">Add
Product</button>
</form>
```

In this updated form:

- The #productForm template reference variable allows you to access the form's validity state.
- The ngIf directives display error messages if the input fields are invalid and have been touched.

Submitting the Form and Handling Errors

When you submit the form, ensure that you handle server-side validation errors as well. Update the onSubmit method in the hello-world.component.ts:

```typescript
Copy code
onSubmit(): void {
  this.productService.addProduct(this.newProduct).subscribe(
    product => {
      this.products.push(product);
      this.newProduct = { id: 0, name: '', price: 0 }; // Reset
      the form
      this.errorMessage = ''; // Clear any previous error messages
    },
    error => {
      if (error.status === 400) {
        this.errorMessage = 'Invalid data submitted. Please check
        your input.';
      } else {
        this.errorMessage = 'An error occurred while adding the
        product.';
      }
    }
```

```
  );
}
```

In this implementation:

- If the server responds with a **400 Bad Request**, you can display a user-friendly error message.
- For other error statuses, provide a generic error message.

Conclusion

In this chapter, you've learned how to effectively integrate your Angular application with the ASP.NET Core Web API. You explored the HTTPClient service for making API requests, handled JSON data, configured CORS for cross-origin requests, and implemented error handling and validation.

Chapter 5: Data Persistence and Database Integration

I n modern web applications, data persistence and management are crucial components that define the overall functionality and user experience. In this chapter, we will explore how to integrate a database with your ASP.NET Core Web API and use Entity Framework Core (EF Core) to handle data access and persistence. We will discuss creating database models, configuring the database context, performing CRUD (Create, Read, Update, Delete) operations, and seeding the database with initial data. By the end of this chapter, you will have a solid understanding of how to manage data in your applications and integrate them effectively with your Angular front end.

Understanding Data Persistence and Database Integration

What is Data Persistence?

Data persistence refers to the ability of data to outlive the application that created it. In other words, it ensures that data is stored in a way that allows it to be retrieved and modified even after the application has closed. Common methods of data persistence include using databases, file systems, or cloud storage services.

Why Use a Database?

Using a database for data persistence offers several advantages:

1. **Structured Data Storage**: Databases provide a structured way to store data, which makes it easy to query and retrieve specific information.
2. **Scalability**: Databases can handle large volumes of data and support multiple concurrent users, making them suitable for modern web applications.
3. **Data Integrity**: Databases enforce rules and constraints to maintain data integrity, ensuring that data remains consistent and accurate.
4. **Security**: Most databases offer built-in security features, allowing you to manage access and permissions to protect sensitive data.

In this chapter, we will focus on using **Entity Framework Core (EF Core)**, a powerful Object-Relational Mapping (ORM) framework that simplifies database interactions in ASP.NET Core applications.

Setting Up Entity Framework Core

1. Installing EF Core

To get started with EF Core, you need to install the required NuGet packages in your ASP.NET Core Web API project.

1. Open the terminal and navigate to your project folder.
2. Run the following command to install EF Core and the SQL Server provider (or any other provider you prefer):

```bash
Copy code
```

```
dotnet add package Microsoft.EntityFrameworkCore
dotnet add package Microsoft.EntityFrameworkCore.SqlServer
dotnet add package Microsoft.EntityFrameworkCore.Tools
```

2. Configuring the Database Context

The **Database Context** is a class that derives from DbContext and serves as a bridge between your application and the database. It manages the database connections and is responsible for querying and saving data.

1. Create a folder named **Data** in your project root.
2. Inside the **Data** folder, create a class named ApplicationDbContext.cs.

```csharp
Copy code
using Microsoft.EntityFrameworkCore;
using MyFirstApi.Models;

namespace MyFirstApi.Data
{
    public class ApplicationDbContext : DbContext
    {
        public ApplicationDbContext(DbContextOptions
<ApplicationDbContext> options)
            : base(options)
        {
        }

        public DbSet<Product> Products { get; set; }
    }
}
```

3. Configuring Connection Strings

To connect to the database, you need to define a connection string in your appsettings.json file.

1. Open the appsettings.json file and add a connection string:

```json
Copy code
{
  "ConnectionStrings": {
    "DefaultConnection": "Server=
(localdb)\\mssqllocaldb;Database=
MyFirstApiDb;Trusted_Connection=True;"
  },
  "Logging": {
    "LogLevel": {
      "Default": "Information",
      "Microsoft": "Warning",
      "Microsoft.Hosting.Lifetime": "Information"
    }
  },
  "AllowedHosts": "*"
}
```

4. Registering the Database Context

Next, register the database context in the Startup.cs file.

1. Open Startup.cs and modify the ConfigureServices method:

```csharp
csharp
Copy code
using Microsoft.EntityFrameworkCore;
using MyFirstApi.Data;

public void ConfigureServices(IServiceCollection services)
{
    services.AddDbContext<ApplicationDbContext>(options =>
        options.UseSqlServer(Configuration.
GetConnectionString("DefaultConnection")));

    services.AddControllers();
    services.AddCors(options =>
    {
        options.AddPolicy("AllowAllOrigins",
            builder =>
            {
                builder.AllowAnyOrigin()
                       .AllowAnyMethod()
                       .AllowAnyHeader();
            });
    });
}
```

5. Enabling Migrations

EF Core uses migrations to create and update the database schema. To enable migrations, run the following command in the terminal:

```bash
bash
Copy code
dotnet ef migrations add InitialCreate
```

This command creates a new migration named **InitialCreate** based on the current model (the Product class in this case).

6. Updating the Database

To apply the migration and create the database, run the following command:

```bash
Copy code
dotnet ef database update
```

This command will create a new database based on the connection string you provided, and it will create the necessary tables based on your model.

Creating Database Models

Defining the Product Model

We have already defined the Product model earlier, but let's review it to ensure it's correctly set up for data persistence.

```csharp
Copy code
using System.ComponentModel.DataAnnotations;

namespace MyFirstApi.Models
{
    public class Product
    {
        public int Id { get; set; }

        [Required(ErrorMessage = "Name is required.")]
        [StringLength(100, ErrorMessage =
"Name cannot exceed 100 characters.")]
        public string Name { get; set; }

        [Range(0.01, double.MaxValue,
ErrorMessage = "Price must be greater than 0.")]
        public decimal Price { get; set; }
```

```csharp
        public string Description { get; set; }
    }
}
```

Seeding the Database with Initial Data

Seeding the database allows you to populate it with initial data for testing or demonstration purposes. To seed the database, you can override the OnModelCreating method in your ApplicationDbContext.

1. Update the ApplicationDbContext.cs file:

```csharp
csharp
Copy code
using Microsoft.EntityFrameworkCore;
using MyFirstApi.Models;

namespace MyFirstApi.Data
{
    public class ApplicationDbContext : DbContext
    {
        public ApplicationDbContext(DbContextOptions
<ApplicationDbContext> options)
            : base(options)
        {
        }

        public DbSet<Product>
 Products { get; set; }

        protected override void
OnModelCreating(ModelBuilder modelBuilder)
        {
```

```
        modelBuilder.Entity<Product>().HasData(
new Product { Id = 1, Name = "Product1",
Price = 19.99M, Description =
"Description for Product1" },
new Product { Id = 2, Name =
"Product2", Price = 29.99M,
Description = "Description for Product2" },
new Product { Id = 3, Name =
"Product3", Price = 39.99M,
Description = "Description for Product3" }
            );
        }
    }
}
```

Updating the Database Again

After seeding the data, you need to create a new migration and update the database again:

1. Run the following commands:

```bash
Copy code
dotnet ef migrations add SeedData
dotnet ef database update
```

Now, the database should be populated with the initial product data.

Performing CRUD Operations

Now that we have set up the database and seeded it with initial data, let's implement the CRUD operations in our **ProductsController**.

1. Creating a Product

To create a new product, add a POST method to your ProductsController:

```csharp
Copy code
[HttpPost]
public ActionResult<Product> AddProduct(Product product)
{
    if (!ModelState.IsValid)
    {
        return BadRequest(ModelState);
    }

    _context.Products.Add(product);
    _context.SaveChanges();

    return CreatedAtAction
(nameof(GetProductById),
new { id = product.Id }, product);
}
```

2. Reading Products

The existing GET method for retrieving all products can be reused:

```csharp
Copy code
[HttpGet]
public ActionResult<IEnumerable
<Product>> GetProducts()
{
    return _context.Products.ToList();
}
```

You can also implement a method to get a product by ID:

```csharp
Copy code
[HttpGet("{id}")]
public ActionResult<Product> GetProductById(int id)
{
    var product = _context.Products.Find(id);

    if (product == null)
    {
        return NotFound();
    }

    return product;
}
```

3. Updating a Product

To update an existing product, you can add a PUT method:

```csharp
Copy code
[HttpPut("{id}")]
public ActionResult<Product>
UpdateProduct(int id, Product product)
{
    if (id != product.Id || !ModelState.IsValid)
    {
        return BadRequest(ModelState);
    }

    _context.Entry(product).State = EntityState.Modified;
    _context.SaveChanges();

    return NoContent();
}
```

4. Deleting a Product

To delete a product, add a DELETE method:

```csharp
Copy code
[HttpDelete("{id}")]
public ActionResult DeleteProduct(int id)
{
    var product = _context.Products.Find(id);

    if (product == null)
    {
        return NotFound();
    }

    _context.Products.Remove(product);
    _context.SaveChanges();

    return NoContent();
}
```

Testing CRUD Operations

Now that we have implemented the CRUD operations in the controller, you can test them using tools like **Postman** or **curl**.

Using Postman

1. **GET Products**: Send a GET request to https://localhost:5001/api/products.
2. **Add Product**: Send a POST request to https://localhost:5001/api/products with a JSON body:

```json
Copy code
{
  "name": "New Product",
  "price": 25.00,
  "description": "This is a new product."
}
```

1. **Update Product**: Send a PUT request to https://localhost:5001/api/p roducts/{id} with a JSON body:

```json
Copy code
{
  "id": 1,
  "name": "Updated Product",
  "price": 30.00,
  "description": "This is an updated product."
}
```

1. **Delete Product**: Send a DELETE request to https://localhost:5001/ap i/products/{id}.

Integrating Angular with the Database

Now that we have a fully functional API, let's integrate it with our Angular application.

Fetching Products in Angular

1. Open the hello-world.component.ts file and ensure the service method is called when the component initializes:

```typescript
Copy code
ngOnInit(): void {
  this.productService.getProducts().subscribe(
    data => {
      this.products = data;
    },
    error => {
      this.errorMessage = error;
    }
  );
}
```

Creating a Product in Angular

To add functionality for creating a product, modify the form in hello-world. component.html:

```html
Copy code
<form (ngSubmit)="onSubmit()" #productForm="ngForm">
  <input type="text" [(ngModel)]=
"newProduct.name" name="name"
 placeholder="Product Name" required>
  <div *ngIf="productForm.controls.name?.invalid &&
  productForm.controls.name?.touched">
    <small class="error">Product
 Name is required.</small>
  </div>
```

```
<input type="number" [(ngModel)]=
"newProduct.price" name="price"
placeholder="Product Price" required>
  <div *ngIf="productForm.controls.price?.invalid &&
  productForm.controls.price?.touched">
    <small class="error">
Price must be greater than 0.</small>
  </div>

  <button type="submit"
[disabled]="productForm.invalid">Add Product</button>
</form>
```

Handling Form Submission

In the hello-world.component.ts, implement the logic for form submission:

```typescript
Copy code
onSubmit(): void {
  this.productService.addProduct
(this.newProduct).subscribe(
    product => {
      this.products.push(product);
      this.newProduct =
{ id: 0, name: '', price: 0 }; // Reset the form
      this.errorMessage = '';
// Clear any previous error messages
    },
    error => {
      if (error.status === 400) {
        this.errorMessage =
'Invalid data submitted. Please check your input.';
      } else {
        this.errorMessage = 'An error occurred while adding the
        product.';
```

```
        }
      }
    );
}
```

Updating and Deleting Products in Angular

To implement updating and deleting functionality, you can create buttons in the template to handle these actions:

```html
html
Copy code
<ul>
  <li *ngFor="let product of products">
    {{ product.name }} - ${{ product.price }}
    <button (click)="editProduct
(product)">Edit</button>
    <button (click)="deleteProduct
(product.id)">Delete</button>
  </li>
</ul>
```

In the hello-world.component.ts, implement the editProduct and deleteProduct methods:

```typescript
typescript
Copy code
editProduct(product: Product): void {
  // Logic for editing a product
(show a modal or populate the form)
}

deleteProduct(id: number): void {
  this.productService.deleteProduct(id).subscribe(
    () => {
```

```
      this.products = this.products.filter(p => p.id !== id);
      this.errorMessage = '';
// Clear any previous error messages
    },
    error => {
      this.errorMessage =
'An error occurred while deleting the product.';
    }
  );
}
```

Conclusion

In this chapter, we explored data persistence and database integration in your ASP.NET Core Web API. We learned how to set up Entity Framework Core, create a database context, define models, and perform CRUD operations. Additionally, we integrated our API with the Angular front end, allowing us to fetch, create, update, and delete products seamlessly.

Chapter 6: Authentication and Authorization

In modern web applications, ensuring that users are who they say they are (authentication) and controlling what they can do (authorization) is critical for security. This chapter focuses on implementing authentication and authorization in your ASP.NET Core Web API and integrating it with your Angular application.

We will cover the following topics:

1. Understanding authentication and authorization.
2. Implementing JWT (JSON Web Token) authentication in ASP.NET Core.
3. Securing your ASP.NET Core API endpoints.
4. Integrating authentication in your Angular application.
5. Protecting routes and managing user sessions.

By the end of this chapter, you will have a solid foundation for implementing security in your full-stack applications.

Understanding Authentication and Authorization

What is Authentication?

Authentication is the process of verifying the identity of a user or system. It ensures that the entity requesting access to the system is indeed who they claim to be. Common authentication methods include:

- **Username and Password**: The most traditional method where users enter their credentials to gain access.
- **Multi-Factor Authentication (MFA)**: An additional layer of security requiring two or more verification factors (e.g., a password and a text message code).
- **OAuth**: A protocol that allows applications to access user data without exposing their passwords (commonly used with third-party login options).

What is Authorization?

Authorization, on the other hand, determines whether an authenticated user has permission to access specific resources or perform certain actions. It is crucial for enforcing security policies and controlling access to data and functionality within an application.

Authorization can be role-based (RBAC), where users are assigned roles (e.g., admin, user, guest) with specific permissions, or attribute-based (ABAC), where access is granted based on user attributes and environmental factors.

The Relationship Between Authentication and Authorization

Authentication and authorization work together to secure applications. A user must first be authenticated before authorization can be applied. For example, an application might allow only authenticated users to view specific pages, but only those with the "admin" role to access administrative features.

Implementing JWT Authentication in ASP.NET Core

What is JWT?

JWT (JSON Web Token) is a compact, URL-safe means of representing claims to be transferred between two parties. The claims in a JWT are encoded as a JSON object that is used as the payload of a JSON Web Signature (JWS) structure or as the plaintext of a JSON Web Encryption (JWE) structure, enabling the claims to be digitally signed or integrity protected with a message authentication code.

A typical JWT is composed of three parts:

1. **Header**: Contains metadata about the token, including the type of token and the signing algorithm.
2. **Payload**: Contains the claims, which are statements about the user (e.g., user ID, roles).
3. **Signature**: Used to verify that the sender of the JWT is who it claims to be and to ensure that the message wasn't changed along the way.

Setting Up JWT Authentication

1. Install Required NuGet Packages

To implement JWT authentication in your ASP.NET Core Web API, you need to install the following NuGet package:

```bash
Copy code
dotnet add package Microsoft.AspNetCore.
Authentication.JwtBearer
```

2. Configure JWT Authentication in Startup.cs

Open the Startup.cs file and modify it to configure JWT authentication.

1. Add the following using directives at the top of the file:

81

```csharp
Copy code
using Microsoft.AspNetCore.Authentication.JwtBearer;
using Microsoft.IdentityModel.Tokens;
using System.Text;
```

1. Update the ConfigureServices method to configure authentication services:

```csharp
Copy code
public void ConfigureServices
(IServiceCollection services)
{
    services.AddDbContext<
ApplicationDbContext>(options =>
        options.UseSqlServer(Configuration.
GetConnectionString("DefaultConnection")));

    services.AddControllers();

    // JWT Authentication configuration
    var key = Encoding.ASCII.GetBytes
(Configuration["Jwt:Key"]);
    services.AddAuthentication(x =>
    {
        x.DefaultAuthenticateScheme =
        JwtBearerDefaults.AuthenticationScheme;
        x.DefaultChallengeScheme =
        JwtBearerDefaults.AuthenticationScheme;
    })
    .AddJwtBearer(x =>
    {
        x.RequireHttpsMetadata = true;
```

```
        x.SaveToken = true;
        x.TokenValidationParameters =
new TokenValidationParameters
        {
            ValidateIssuerSigningKey = true,
            IssuerSigningKey = new
SymmetricSecurityKey(key),
            ValidateIssuer = false,
            ValidateAudience = false
        };
    });

    services.AddCors(options =>
    {
        options.AddPolicy("AllowAllOrigins",
            builder =>
            {
                builder.AllowAnyOrigin()
                    .AllowAnyMethod()
                    .AllowAnyHeader();
            });
    });
}
```

In this configuration:

- The JWT key is retrieved from the configuration.
- The token validation parameters are set to validate the signing key and to allow any issuer and audience.

3. Configure JWT Settings in appsettings.json

Next, add the JWT settings to your appsettings.json file:

```json
Copy code
{
  "Jwt": {
```

```
    "Key": "Your_Secret_Key_Here", //
  Replace with a secure key
    "Issuer": "YourIssuer"
  },
  // other configurations...
}
```

Make sure to replace "Your_Secret_Key_Here" with a strong, secure key.

4. Generating JWT Tokens

You need to create a method to generate JWT tokens after successful authentication. Let's create an AuthController for handling user authentication.

1. Create a new controller named AuthController.cs in the **Controllers** folder.
2. Add the following code:

```csharp
Copy code
using Microsoft.AspNetCore.Mvc;
using Microsoft.IdentityModel.Tokens;
using System;
using System.Collections.Generic;
using System.IdentityModel.Tokens.Jwt;
using System.Security.Claims;
using System.Text;
using MyFirstApi.Models;

namespace MyFirstApi.Controllers
{
    [Route("api/[controller]")]
    [ApiController]
    public class AuthController : ControllerBase
    {
        [HttpPost("login")]
```

```
        public IActionResult Login
([FromBody] UserLogin userLogin)
        {
            // In a real application, you would validate the user
            credentials with a database
            if (userLogin.Username ==
"admin" && userLogin.Password ==
"password") // Dummy validation
            {
                var tokenHandler =
new JwtSecurityTokenHandler();
                var key = Encoding.ASCII.GetBytes
("Your_Secret_Key_Here");
// Ensure to use the same key as in appsettings
                var tokenDescriptor =
new SecurityTokenDescriptor
                {
Subject = new ClaimsIdentity(new Claim[]
                    {
                        new Claim(ClaimTypes.Name,
                        userLogin.Username)
                    }),
Expires = DateTime.UtcNow.AddDays(7),
SigningCredentials = new SigningCredentials(new
SymmetricSecurityKey(key),
SecurityAlgorithms.HmacSha256Signature)
                };

                var token =
                tokenHandler.CreateToken(tokenDescriptor);
                return Ok(new { Token =
                tokenHandler.WriteToken(token) });
            }

            return Unauthorized();
        }
    }
}
```

User Login Model

Create a model for user login:

1. In the **Models** folder, create a class named UserLogin.cs.

```csharp
Copy code
namespace MyFirstApi.Models
{
    public class UserLogin
    {
        public string Username { get; set; }
        public string Password { get; set; }
    }
}
```

Testing the JWT Authentication

1. Run your ASP.NET Core Web API using:

```bash
Copy code
dotnet run
```

1. Use Postman to send a POST request to the login endpoint:

```bash
Copy code
```

```
POST https://localhost:5001/api/auth/login
Content-Type: application/json

{
    "username": "admin",
    "password": "password"
}
```

1. On a successful login, you should receive a response containing the JWT token:

```
json
Copy code
{
    "token": "your_jwt_token_here"
}
```

5. Securing Your API Endpoints

To protect your API endpoints, you can use the [Authorize] attribute. This ensures that only authenticated users can access certain routes.

1. Update your ProductsController to secure the endpoints:

```csharp
csharp
Copy code
[Authorize]
[Route("api/[controller]")]
[ApiController]
public class ProductsController : ControllerBase
{
```

```
    // Existing code...
}
```

Now, any request to the ProductsController will require a valid JWT token.

6. Configuring Authentication Middleware

To enable authentication, make sure to add the authentication middleware in the Configure method of the Startup.cs file:

```csharp
csharp
Copy code
public void Configure(IApplicationBuilder app,
IWebHostEnvironment env)
{
    if (env.IsDevelopment())
    {
        app.UseDeveloperExceptionPage();
    }

    app.UseHttpsRedirection();

    app.UseRouting();

    app.UseCors("AllowAllOrigins"); // Enable CORS

    app.UseAuthentication(); // Enable authentication
    app.UseAuthorization(); // Enable authorization

    app.UseEndpoints(endpoints =>
    {
        endpoints.MapControllers();
    });
}
```

Integrating Authentication in Your Angular Application

Now that we have set up JWT authentication in the ASP.NET Core API, let's integrate it with the Angular application.

1. Creating an Authentication Service

In your Angular application, create an authentication service that will handle login and token management.

1. Generate a new service using Angular CLI:

```bash
Copy code
ng generate service auth
```

1. Update the auth.service.ts file:

```typescript
Copy code
import { Injectable } from '@angular/core';
import { HttpClient } from '@angular/common/http';
import { Observable } from 'rxjs';
import { tap } from 'rxjs/operators';

@Injectable({
  providedIn: 'root'
})
export class AuthService {
  private apiUrl = 'https://localhost:5001/api/auth';
  private token: string | null = null;
```

```
  constructor(private http: HttpClient) { }

  login(username: string, password: string):
 Observable<any> {
    return this.http.post<any>
(`${this.apiUrl}/login`, { username, password }).pipe(
      tap(response => {
        this.token = response.token;
        localStorage.setItem
('jwt', this.token); // Store token in local storage
      })
    );
  }

  logout(): void {
    this.token = null;
    localStorage.removeItem('jwt');
// Remove token from local storage
  }

  isAuthenticated(): boolean {
    return this.token != null; // Check if token exists
  }
}
```

2. Creating a Login Component

Next, let's create a login component that allows users to authenticate themselves.

1. Generate a new component using Angular CLI:

```bash
bash
Copy code
```

```
ng generate component login
```

1. Update the login.component.ts file:

```typescript
Copy code
import { Component } from '@angular/core';
import { AuthService } from '../auth.service';

@Component({
  selector: 'app-login',
  templateUrl: './login.component.html',
  styleUrls: ['./login.component.css']
})
export class LoginComponent {
  username: string = '';
  password: string = '';
  errorMessage: string = '';

  constructor(private authService: AuthService) { }

  onSubmit(): void {
    this.authService.login(this.username,
this.password).subscribe(
      response => {
        console.log('Login successful!', response);
        // Redirect or perform
actions after successful login
      },
      error => {
        this.errorMessage = 'Invalid username or password';
      }
    );
  }
}
```

3. Login Template

Update the login.component.html file to include a simple form:

```html
Copy code
<form (ngSubmit)="onSubmit()">
  <div>
    <label for="username">Username</label>
    <input type="text" id="username"
 [(ngModel)]="username" name="username" required>
  </div>
  <div>
    <label for="password">Password</label>
    <input type="password" id=
"password" [(ngModel)]=
"password" name="password" required>
  </div>
  <button type="submit">Login</button>
  <div *ngIf="errorMessage"
 class="error">{{ errorMessage }}</div>
</form>
```

4. Protecting Routes with Guards

To protect certain routes in your Angular application, you can create a route guard that checks if the user is authenticated before allowing access.

1. Generate a new guard using Angular CLI:

```bash
Copy code
ng generate guard auth
```

1. Update the generated auth.guard.ts file:

```typescript
Copy code
import { Injectable } from '@angular/core';
import { CanActivate, Router } from '@angular/router';
import { AuthService } from './auth.service';

@Injectable({
  providedIn: 'root'
})
export class AuthGuard implements CanActivate {
  constructor(private authService:
 AuthService, private router: Router) { }

  canActivate(): boolean {
    if (this.authService.isAuthenticated()) {
      return true;
    } else {
      this.router.navigate(['/login']);
      return false;
    }
  }
}
```

5. Applying the Guard to Routes

To use the guard, apply it to your routes in the app-routing.module.ts file:

```typescript
Copy code
import { AuthGuard } from './auth.guard';

const routes: Routes = [
  { path: 'hello', component:
```

```
  HelloWorldComponent, canActivate: [AuthGuard] },
  { path: 'login', component: LoginComponent },
  { path: '', redirectTo: '/hello', pathMatch: 'full' }
];
```

6. Managing User Sessions

With authentication implemented, you can manage user sessions by checking the token stored in local storage. This can be done in the AuthService.

1. Update the AuthService to check for the token:

```typescript
Copy code
isAuthenticated(): boolean {
  this.token = localStorage.getItem('jwt');
  return this.token != null;
}
```

7. Adding Logout Functionality

Implement the logout feature in your application. You can create a logout button in your navigation bar:

```html
Copy code
<button (click)="authService.
logout()">Logout</button>
```

In the component that includes the navigation, you can check if the user is authenticated to show or hide the logout button:

```html
html
Copy code
<nav>
  <a routerLink="/hello">Products</a>
  <a routerLink="/login"
  *ngIf="!authService.isAuthenticated()">Login</a>
  <button *ngIf="authService.isAuthenticated()"
  (click)="authService.logout()">Logout</button>
</nav>
```

Conclusion

In this chapter, you learned how to implement authentication and authorization in your ASP.NET Core Web API and integrate it with your Angular application. You explored the concept of JWT (JSON Web Tokens) for secure authentication, configured your API to use JWT, and built an Angular service to manage user login and sessions.

By following these steps, you have set a strong foundation for securing your full-stack application. In the next chapter, we will delve deeper into advanced Angular features such as routing, guards, and lazy loading to enhance the user experience further.

Chapter 7: Advanced Angular Features

As you progress in building your Angular application, understanding advanced features becomes crucial for creating a robust, scalable, and user-friendly experience. This chapter delves into several advanced concepts in Angular, including:

1. Angular Routing and Navigation
2. Route Guards
3. Lazy Loading Modules
4. Managing State with Services
5. Creating Custom Directives and Pipes
6. Advanced Component Interaction
7. Using Angular Forms for Complex Scenarios

By the end of this chapter, you will have a deeper understanding of Angular's capabilities and how to implement them effectively in your application.

Angular Routing and Navigation

Understanding Angular Routing

Routing in Angular allows you to navigate between different views or components in a single-page application (SPA) without refreshing the entire page. The Angular Router enables developers to define routes, associate them with components, and manage navigation within the application.

Setting Up Angular Routing

To begin using routing in your Angular application, you need to ensure that the Angular Router is properly configured.

1. Importing RouterModule

If you haven't already set up routing in your Angular application, you can do so by modifying the app-routing.module.ts file. If this file doesn't exist, create it in the src/app folder:

```bash
Copy code
ng generate module app-routing --flat --module=app
```

Open the app-routing.module.ts file and set up the basic routing:

```typescript
Copy code
import { NgModule } from '@angular/core';
import { RouterModule, Routes } from '@angular/router';
import { HelloWorldComponent } from
'./hello-world/hello-world.component';
import { LoginComponent } from './login/login.component';

const routes: Routes = [
  { path: 'hello', component: HelloWorldComponent },
  { path: 'login', component: LoginComponent },
  { path: '', redirectTo: '/hello', pathMatch: 'full' },
  { path: '**', redirectTo: '/hello' } // Wildcard route for a
```

```
   404 page
];

@NgModule({
  imports: [RouterModule.forRoot(routes)],
  exports: [RouterModule]
})
export class AppRoutingModule { }
```

In this routing setup:

- We defined a route for HelloWorldComponent and LoginComponent.
- The redirectTo property is used to redirect users to the default route when they access the root URL (/).
- The wildcard route (path: '**') catches all undefined routes, redirecting them to the hello route.

2. Adding Router Links

To enable navigation between components, use the routerLink directive in your templates. For example, in your app.component.html, you might have:

```html
Copy code
<nav>
  <a routerLink="/hello">Products</a>
  <a routerLink="/login">Login</a>
</nav>

<router-outlet></router-outlet>
```

The <router-outlet> directive is where the routed components will be displayed based on the current URL.

3. Navigating Programmatically

In addition to using routerLink, you can navigate programmatically using the Angular Router service. Inject the Router in your component:

```typescript
Copy code
import { Component } from '@angular/core';
import { Router } from '@angular/router';

@Component({
  // Component metadata
})
export class SomeComponent {
  constructor(private router: Router) { }

  navigateToHello(): void {
    this.router.navigate(['/hello']);
  }
}
```

This method is particularly useful for navigating after performing an action, such as logging in or submitting a form.

4. Route Parameters

In many applications, you need to pass parameters in the route to identify resources. To define a route with parameters, use the colon (:) syntax.

Example: Defining a Route with Parameters

Modify the routing configuration to include a parameter for product details:

```typescript
Copy code
{ path: 'product/:id', component: ProductDetailComponent }
```

In the ProductDetailComponent, you can access the route parameters using the ActivatedRoute service:

```typescript
Copy code
import { Component, OnInit } from '@angular/core';
import { ActivatedRoute } from '@angular/router';

@Component({
  // Component metadata
})
export class ProductDetailComponent implements OnInit {
  productId: number;

  constructor(private route: ActivatedRoute) { }

  ngOnInit(): void {
    this.productId = +this.route.snapshot.paramMap.get('id'); //
    Get the ID parameter
  }
}
```

The ActivatedRoute service allows you to retrieve the current route parameters, which you can use to fetch data from the API or perform other actions.

Route Guards

What are Route Guards?

Route guards are a feature in Angular that enables you to control access to routes based on specific conditions. They are useful for implementing security measures, such as preventing unauthorized users from accessing certain parts of your application.

Types of Route Guards

Angular provides several types of route guards:

1. **CanActivate**: Determines whether a route can be activated.
2. **CanDeactivate**: Determines whether a user can navigate away from a route.
3. **Resolve**: Pre-fetches data before activating a route.
4. **CanLoad**: Determines whether a module can be loaded.

Implementing CanActivate Guard

Let's implement a CanActivate guard to protect routes that require authentication.

1. If you haven't already created a guard, generate one using Angular CLI:

```bash
Copy code
ng generate guard auth
```

1. Update the generated auth.guard.ts file:

```typescript
Copy code
import { Injectable } from '@angular/core';
import { CanActivate, Router } from '@angular/router';
import { AuthService } from './auth.service';

@Injectable({
```

```
    providedIn: 'root'
})
export class AuthGuard implements CanActivate {
  constructor(private authService: AuthService, private router:
  Router) { }

  canActivate(): boolean {
    if (this.authService.isAuthenticated()) {
      return true; // User is authenticated, allow access
    } else {
      this.router.navigate(['/login']); // Redirect to login
      return false; // User is not authenticated, deny access
    }
  }
}
```

Using the Guard in Routing

Apply the guard to routes in your app-routing.module.ts:

```typescript
Copy code
const routes: Routes = [
  { path: 'hello', component: HelloWorldComponent, canActivate:
  [AuthGuard] },
  { path: 'login', component: LoginComponent },
  { path: '', redirectTo: '/hello', pathMatch: 'full' }
];
```

With this configuration, the hello route will only be accessible to authenticated users.

Lazy Loading Modules

What is Lazy Loading?

Lazy loading is a design pattern that improves application performance by loading modules only when they are needed. This reduces the initial load time of your application, which is especially beneficial for larger applications.

Implementing Lazy Loading

To implement lazy loading in Angular, follow these steps:

1. Create a new feature module using Angular CLI:

```bash
Copy code
ng generate module feature --route feature --module app.module
```

This command creates a new module and configures it for lazy loading.

1. The command will automatically update your routing configuration to include the lazy-loaded route:

```typescript
Copy code
const routes: Routes = [
  { path: 'feature', loadChildren: () =>
  import('./feature/feature.module').then(m => m.FeatureModule) }
];
```

Creating the Feature Module

In the feature directory, you can create components and services specific to that module. For example, create a new component within the feature module:

```bash
bash
Copy code
ng generate component feature/my-feature
```

Setting Up Routing in the Feature Module

Create a new routing module for the feature:

1. Generate the routing module:

```bash
bash
Copy code
ng generate module feature/feature-routing --flat --module=feature
```

1. Define routes in the feature-routing.module.ts file:

```typescript
typescript
Copy code
import { NgModule } from '@angular/core';
import { RouterModule, Routes } from '@angular/router';
import { MyFeatureComponent } from
'./my-feature/my-feature.component';
```

```
const routes: Routes = [
  { path: '', component: MyFeatureComponent } // Default route
  for feature
];

@NgModule({
  imports: [RouterModule.forChild(routes)],
  exports: [RouterModule]
})
export class FeatureRoutingModule { }
```

Accessing Lazy Loaded Modules

With lazy loading set up, you can access the feature module by navigating to the corresponding URL (e.g., /feature). The module and its components will only be loaded when the user navigates to that route, improving the initial load performance of your application.

Managing State with Services

Understanding State Management

In a typical application, you often need to manage the state of various components, especially in large applications. Angular services are an effective way to manage state across components. Services allow you to share data between different parts of your application and maintain a single source of truth.

Creating a State Management Service

1. Generate a new service for state management:

```bash
bash
Copy code
ng generate service state
```

1. Update the state.service.ts file:

```typescript
typescript
Copy code
import { Injectable } from '@angular/core';
import { BehaviorSubject } from 'rxjs';
import { Product } from './models/product.model';

@Injectable({
  providedIn: 'root'
})
export class StateService {
  private productsSource = new BehaviorSubject<Product[]>([]);
  currentProducts = this.productsSource.asObservable();

  constructor() { }

  changeProducts(products: Product[]): void {
    this.productsSource.next(products);
  }
}
```

Using the State Management Service in Components

In any component where you want to access the state:

1. Inject the StateService:

```typescript
Copy code
import { Component, OnInit } from '@angular/core';
import { StateService } from '../state.service';
import { Product } from '../models/product.model';

@Component({
  // Component metadata
})
export class SomeComponent implements OnInit {
  products: Product[];

  constructor(private stateService: StateService) { }

  ngOnInit(): void {
    this.stateService.currentProducts.subscribe(products => {
      this.products = products;
    });
  }
}
```

Updating the State

When you update the products (e.g., after adding or removing a product), you can call the changeProducts method from your service to update the state:

```typescript
Copy code
this.stateService.changeProducts(updatedProducts);
```

This ensures that any component subscribing to the currentProducts observable will automatically receive the updated data.

Creating Custom Directives and Pipes

What are Directives?

Directives are classes that can modify the behavior or appearance of DOM elements. Angular provides several built-in directives (like ngFor and ngIf), but you can also create custom directives to encapsulate common functionality.

Creating a Custom Directive

1. Generate a new directive:

```bash
Copy code
ng generate directive highlight
```

1. Update the generated highlight.directive.ts file:

```typescript
Copy code
import { Directive, ElementRef, HostListener } from
'@angular/core';

@Directive({
  selector: '[appHighlight]'
})
export class HighlightDirective {
  constructor(private el: ElementRef) { }

  @HostListener('mouseenter') onMouseEnter() {
    this.highlight('yellow');
```

```
  }

  @HostListener('mouseleave') onMouseLeave() {
    this.highlight(null);
  }

  private highlight(color: string) {
    this.el.nativeElement.style.backgroundColor = color;
  }
}
```

Using the Custom Directive in Templates

To use the HighlightDirective, simply add the appHighlight attribute to any HTML element:

```html
Copy code
<p appHighlight>This text will be highlighted on hover!</p>
```

What are Pipes?

Pipes allow you to transform data in your templates. Angular comes with several built-in pipes (like DatePipe, CurrencyPipe, etc.), but you can create custom pipes to meet specific requirements.

Creating a Custom Pipe

1. Generate a new pipe:

```bash
bash
Copy code
ng generate pipe customCurrency
```

1. Update the generated custom-currency.pipe.ts file:

```typescript
typescript
Copy code
import { Pipe, PipeTransform } from '@angular/core';

@Pipe({
  name: 'customCurrency'
})
export class CustomCurrencyPipe implements PipeTransform {
    transform(value: number, currencySymbol: string = '$'): string {
      return `${currencySymbol}${value.toFixed(2)}`;
    }
}
```

Using the Custom Pipe in Templates

To use the custom pipe, simply apply it in your template:

```html
html
Copy code
<p>The price is: {{ product.price | customCurrency€:'' }}</p>
```

Advanced Component Interaction

Parent-Child Communication with @Input and @Output

Angular provides decorators @Input() and @Output() to facilitate communication between parent and child components.

1. **@Input()** allows a parent component to pass data to a child component.
2. **@Output()** allows a child component to emit events to a parent component.

Example of Parent-Child Communication

1. In the child component, use @Input() to receive data:

```typescript
Copy code
import { Component, Input } from '@angular/core';

@Component({
  selector: 'app-child',
  template: `<p>{{ childData }}</p>`
})
export class ChildComponent {
  @Input() childData: string;
}
```

1. In the parent component, use @Output() to emit an event:

```typescript
Copy code
import { Component, EventEmitter, Output } from '@angular/core';

@Component({
```

```
  selector: 'app-parent',
  template: `
    <app-child [childData]="parentData"></app-child>
    <button (click)="sendData()">Send Data</button>
  `
})
export class ParentComponent {
  parentData = 'Hello from Parent';

  @Output() dataSent = new EventEmitter<string>();

  sendData() {
    this.dataSent.emit('Data from Parent');
  }
}
```

Using Content Projection

Content projection allows you to create reusable components that can accept external content. This is achieved using the <ng-content> directive.

Example of Content Projection

1. In a component, use <ng-content>:

```
typescript
Copy code
import { Component } from '@angular/core';

@Component({
  selector: 'app-card',
  template: `
    <div class="card">
      <ng-content></ng-content>
    </div>
  `,
```

```
styles: [`
  .card {
    border: 1px solid #ccc;
    padding: 16px;
  }
  `]
})
export class CardComponent {}
```

1. Use the component with content:

```html
Copy code
<app-card>
  <h2>Card Title</h2>
  <p>This is some content inside the card.</p>
</app-card>
```

Managing Component State with Services

In large applications, managing the state across multiple components can become complex. Using Angular services to manage application state provides a centralized way to maintain data and behavior.

1. Create a service for managing the application state (as shown previously).
2. Inject this service into any component that needs access to the shared state.

Conclusion

In this chapter, we explored advanced Angular features that enhance your application's functionality and user experience. We covered routing and navigation, implemented route guards for security, utilized lazy loading for better performance, managed application state using services, and created custom directives and pipes for reusable functionality.

By mastering these concepts, you are now equipped to create more complex and scalable Angular applications. In the next chapter, we will delve into testing in Angular and ASP.NET Core, ensuring that your application is robust and maintainable.

Chapter 8: Testing in Angular and ASP.NET Core

Testing is a fundamental aspect of software development that ensures your application functions as expected and maintains a high level of quality. This chapter will cover testing strategies for both Angular and ASP.NET Core, including unit testing, integration testing, and end-to-end testing. By the end of this chapter, you will have a comprehensive understanding of how to implement effective testing in your full-stack applications.

The Importance of Testing

1. Ensuring Code Quality

Testing helps identify bugs and issues in your code early in the development process, allowing you to fix them before they reach production. This leads to higher-quality software and reduces the cost and effort required for debugging later.

2. Facilitating Refactoring

With a robust suite of tests in place, you can confidently refactor your code, knowing that the tests will catch any regressions or new bugs introduced during the process.

3. Supporting Continuous Integration and Deployment (CI/CD)

Automated tests are a crucial part of CI/CD pipelines. They help ensure that new code changes do not break existing functionality, allowing for faster and safer deployments.

4. Improving Collaboration

Testing encourages better collaboration between team members by providing clear documentation of how components are expected to behave. This clarity can improve communication and reduce misunderstandings.

Testing in Angular

1. Setting Up Testing Frameworks

Angular uses Jasmine as its testing framework and Karma as its test runner by default. These tools are integrated into the Angular CLI, making it easy to write and execute tests.

Installing Required Packages

If you set up your Angular project using the CLI, Jasmine and Karma are already included. If you need to install them manually, you can run:

```bash
Copy code
npm install --save-dev jasmine-core
karma karma-jasmine karma-chrome-launcher
```

2. Unit Testing Components

Unit testing focuses on testing individual components in isolation. In Angular, you can create tests for components, services, and pipes.

Example: Testing a Component

1. Open the hello-world.component.spec.ts file, which is created automatically when you generate a component.
2. Write tests for the HelloWorldComponent:

```typescript
Copy code
import { ComponentFixture, TestBed }
 from '@angular/core/testing';
import { HelloWorldComponent } from
'./hello-world.component';

describe('HelloWorldComponent', () => {
  let component: HelloWorldComponent;
  let fixture: ComponentFixture<HelloWorldComponent>;

  beforeEach(async () => {
    await TestBed.configureTestingModule({
      declarations: [ HelloWorldComponent ]
    })
    .compileComponents();
  });

  beforeEach(() => {
    fixture = TestBed.createComponent(HelloWorldComponent);
    component = fixture.componentInstance;
    fixture.detectChanges();
  });

  it('should create', () => {
    expect(component).toBeTruthy();
```

```
  });

  it('should display the message', () => {
    component.message = 'Hello, Angular!';
    fixture.detectChanges();
    const compiled = fixture.nativeElement;
    expect(compiled.querySelector('h1').
 textContent).toContain('Hello, Angular!');
  });
});
```

3. Running Unit Tests

You can run your Angular unit tests using the Angular CLI:

```
bash
Copy code
ng test
```

This command will open a browser and run your tests, displaying the results in the terminal.

4. Testing Services

To test a service, you typically need to provide any dependencies the service has, such as HTTP clients.

Example: Testing a Service

1. Open the product.service.spec.ts file.
2. Write tests for the ProductService:

```typescript
Copy code
import { TestBed } from '@angular/core/testing';
import { HttpClientTestingModule,
 HttpTestingController } from
'@angular/common/http/testing';
import { ProductService } from './product.service';
import { Product } from './models/product.model';

describe('ProductService', () => {
  let service: ProductService;
  let httpMock: HttpTestingController;

  beforeEach(() => {
    TestBed.configureTestingModule({
      imports: [HttpClientTestingModule],
      providers: [ProductService]
    });

    service = TestBed.inject(ProductService);
    httpMock = TestBed.inject(HttpTestingController);
  });

  it('should fetch products', () => {
    const dummyProducts: Product[] = [
      { id: 1, name: 'Product 1', price: 100 },
      { id: 2, name: 'Product 2', price: 200 }
    ];

    service.getProducts().subscribe(products => {
      expect(products.length).toBe(2);
      expect(products).toEqual(dummyProducts);
    });

    const request = httpMock.expectOne
(`${service.apiUrl}`);
    expect(request.request.method).toBe('GET');
    request.flush(dummyProducts);
  });
```

```
afterEach(() => {
    httpMock.verify();
  });
});
```

5. End-to-End Testing with Protractor

Protractor is an end-to-end testing framework for Angular applications. It allows you to test the application as a user would by interacting with the UI.

Setting Up Protractor

If Protractor is not already installed in your project, you can install it by running:

```bash
Copy code
npm install --save-dev protractor
```

After installation, you can run Protractor with the following command:

```bash
Copy code
ng e2e
```

Writing E2E Tests

Create a new spec file in the e2e/src folder. For example, you can create app.e2e-spec.ts:

```typescript
Copy code
import { browser, by, element } from 'protractor';

describe('Angular Application', () => {
```

```
it('should display the Products page', () => {
  browser.get('/');
  expect(element(by.css('h1')).getText()).
toEqual('Products');
  });

  it('should navigate to the login page', () => {
    element(by.linkText('Login')).click();
    expect(browser.getCurrentUrl())
.toContain('/login');
  });
});
```

Testing in ASP.NET Core

1. Setting Up Testing Frameworks

ASP.NET Core uses **xUnit** as its default testing framework. If you need to create a test project, you can run:

```bash
Copy code
dotnet new xunit -n MyFirstApi.Tests
```

2. Writing Unit Tests for Controllers

In ASP.NET Core, you can write unit tests for your controllers by mocking dependencies.

Example: Testing a Controller

1. Create a test class for your ProductsController in the Tests project:

```csharp
using Microsoft.AspNetCore.Mvc;
using Moq;
using MyFirstApi.Controllers;
using MyFirstApi.Models;
using MyFirstApi.Repositories;
using System.Collections.Generic;
using Xunit;

namespace MyFirstApi.Tests
{
    public class ProductsControllerTests
    {
        private readonly ProductsController _controller;
        private readonly Mock<
IProductRepository> _mockRepo;

        public ProductsControllerTests()
        {
            _mockRepo = new Mock<IProductRepository>();
            _controller = new
ProductsController(_mockRepo.Object);
        }

        [Fact]
        public void GetProducts_ReturnsOkResult()
        {
            // Arrange
            _mockRepo.Setup(repo =>
repo.GetAllProducts()).Returns(GetTestProducts());

            // Act
            var result = _controller.GetProducts();

            // Assert
            var okResult = Assert.
IsType<OkObjectResult>(result);
            var products = Assert.
IsAssignableFrom<IEnumerable
```

```
<Product>>(okResult.Value);
        Assert.Equal(3, products.Count());
    }

    private IEnumerable<Product> GetTestProducts()
    {
        return new List<Product>
        {
            new Product { Id = 1,
Name = "Product1", Price = 19.99M },
            new Product { Id = 2,
Name = "Product2", Price = 29.99M },
            new Product { Id = 3,
Name = "Product3", Price = 39.99M }
        };
    }
}
}
```

3. Running ASP.NET Core Tests

To run your ASP.NET Core tests, navigate to the test project folder in your terminal and run:

```bash
Copy code
dotnet test
```

4. Integration Testing

Integration tests validate the interaction between multiple components in your application. You can create integration tests using WebApplicationFac tory to test your API endpoints.

1. Create an integration test class:

```csharp
Copy code
using Microsoft.AspNetCore.Hosting;
using Microsoft.AspNetCore.Mvc.Testing;
using Microsoft.Extensions.DependencyInjection;
using System.Net.Http;
using System.Threading.Tasks;
using Xunit;

namespace MyFirstApi.Tests
{
    public class ProductsApiIntegrationTests :
    IClassFixture<WebApplicationFactory<Startup>>
    {
        private readonly HttpClient _client;

        public ProductsApiIntegrationTests
(WebApplicationFactory<Startup> factory)
        {
            _client = factory.CreateClient();
        }

        [Fact]
        public async Task GetProducts_
ReturnsSuccessStatusCode()
        {
            var response = await _
client.GetAsync("/api/products");
            response.EnsureSuccessStatusCode();
        }
    }
}
```

Conclusion

In this chapter, you explored the critical aspects of testing in both Angular and ASP.NET Core. You learned about unit testing components and services in Angular, end-to-end testing with Protractor, and testing controllers and integration in ASP.NET Core. By implementing these testing strategies, you can ensure that your applications are robust, maintainable, and capable of providing a seamless user experience.

In the next chapter, we will focus on deploying your full-stack application, covering various hosting options and deployment strategies to get your application live and accessible to users.

Chapter 9: Deploying Your Full-Stack Application

Deploying a web application is the final step in the development process, allowing users to access and interact with your software. In this chapter, we will cover various deployment strategies and options for your full-stack application built with Angular and ASP.NET Core. We will discuss:

1. Preparing your application for deployment.
2. Hosting options for ASP.NET Core applications.
3. Hosting options for Angular applications.
4. Deploying the API and front-end to cloud services.
5. CI/CD pipelines for automated deployments.
6. Securing your deployed application.

By the end of this chapter, you will have a comprehensive understanding of how to deploy your full-stack application efficiently and effectively.

Preparing Your Application for Deployment

1. Building the Application

Before deployment, you need to build your application for production. This process optimizes your code, reduces file sizes, and prepares your application for a live environment.

Building the Angular Application

To build your Angular application, run the following command:

```bash
Copy code
ng build --prod
```

This command compiles your Angular application into an output directory (dist/), generating optimized and minified files ready for deployment.

Building the ASP.NET Core Application

For the ASP.NET Core Web API, you can publish the application using the following command:

```bash
Copy code
dotnet publish -c Release
```

This command creates a release build of your API and outputs it to the bin/Release/net6.0/publish directory (the path may vary depending on your target framework).

2. Configuration for Production

Ensure that your application is properly configured for a production environment:

- **Connection Strings**: Update your appsettings.json to include the production database connection string.

127

- **Environment Variables**: Use environment variables for sensitive information, such as API keys and connection strings.
- **CORS Policies**: Ensure your CORS policy is configured to allow requests from your production domain.

Hosting Options for ASP.NET Core Applications

1. Azure App Service

Azure App Service is a popular platform-as-a-service (PaaS) that allows you to host ASP.NET Core applications easily.

Deploying to Azure App Service

1. **Create an Azure App Service**: Log in to the Azure Portal, navigate to "App Services," and create a new App Service.
2. **Configure Deployment**: In the App Service settings, configure deployment options, such as GitHub Actions, Azure DevOps, or manual deployment using FTP.
3. **Publish Your Application**: Use the Azure CLI or Visual Studio to publish your ASP.NET Core application directly to the Azure App Service.

2. AWS Elastic Beanstalk

AWS Elastic Beanstalk is another PaaS offering that simplifies the deployment of ASP.NET Core applications on the Amazon Web Services (AWS) infrastructure.

Deploying to AWS Elastic Beanstalk

1. **Create an Elastic Beanstalk Application**: Log in to the AWS Management Console and create a new Elastic Beanstalk application.
2. **Configure the Environment**: Choose the platform as "ASP.NET Core" and configure the environment settings, such as instance type and

scaling.

3. **Deploy Your Application**: Use the AWS CLI or the Elastic Beanstalk console to upload and deploy your application.

3. Self-Hosting on a VPS

If you prefer more control over your hosting environment, you can self-host your ASP.NET Core application on a Virtual Private Server (VPS).

Steps to Self-Host

1. **Provision a VPS**: Use providers like DigitalOcean, Linode, or AWS to set up a VPS instance.
2. **Install .NET Runtime**: SSH into your server and install the .NET runtime to run your ASP.NET Core application.
3. **Deploy Your Application**: Transfer your published application files to the server and configure a reverse proxy (e.g., Nginx or Apache) to forward requests to your application.

Hosting Options for Angular Applications

1. GitHub Pages

GitHub Pages is a simple and free hosting option for static websites, making it suitable for Angular applications.

Deploying to GitHub Pages

1. **Build Your Application**: Run ng build —prod to generate the production build.
2. **Create a GitHub Repository**: Create a new repository on GitHub for your Angular application.
3. **Deploy Using the Angular CLI**: You can deploy directly using the Angular CLI by running:

```bash
Copy code
ng add angular-cli-ghpages
ng deploy --base-href
"https://<username>.github.io/<repository-name>/"
```

2. Firebase Hosting

Firebase Hosting is a fast and secure hosting platform for web applications, including Angular applications.

Deploying to Firebase Hosting

1. **Install Firebase CLI**: Install Firebase CLI globally using npm:

```bash
Copy code
npm install -g firebase-tools
```

1. **Initialize Firebase in Your Project**: Run the following command and follow the prompts:

```bash
Copy code
firebase init
```

1. **Build Your Angular Application**: Build your application for production using ng build —prod.

2. **Deploy Your Application**: Deploy to Firebase Hosting using:

```bash
Copy code
firebase deploy
```

3. Netlify

Netlify is another powerful platform for hosting static websites, including Angular applications.

Deploying to Netlify

1. **Build Your Application**: Run ng build —prod to generate the production build.
2. **Create a Netlify Account**: Sign up for a Netlify account and create a new site.
3. **Drag and Drop Deployment**: You can drag and drop your dist folder onto the Netlify dashboard for an easy deployment, or link your GitHub repository for continuous deployment.

Deploying the API and Front-End to Cloud Services

1. Deploying to Azure

To deploy both the ASP.NET Core API and Angular application to Azure, you can use Azure App Service for both.

1. **Create a Resource Group**: In the Azure portal, create a new resource group to manage related resources.
2. **Deploy ASP.NET Core API**: Follow the previous steps to deploy your ASP.NET Core API to Azure App Service.

3. **Deploy Angular Application**: You can also create another App Service for your Angular application or serve it from the same API App Service if it's a single-page application.

2. Deploying to AWS

Similarly, you can use AWS services to deploy both parts of your application:

1. **Create an Elastic Beanstalk Application**: Create an application for your ASP.NET Core API and configure it.
2. **Deploy the API**: Deploy your ASP.NET Core API to Elastic Beanstalk.
3. **Use S3 for Angular**: You can deploy your Angular application to an S3 bucket and configure it for static website hosting. This allows for easy access to your front end and a smooth user experience.

CI/CD Pipelines for Automated Deployments

1. Understanding CI/CD

Continuous Integration (CI) and Continuous Deployment (CD) are practices that automate the integration of code changes from multiple contributors into a shared repository and the deployment of code to production environments.

2. Setting Up CI/CD for Angular and ASP.NET Core

Using GitHub Actions

1. **Create a Workflow File**: In your repository, create a .github/workflows/ci.yml file.

```yaml
yaml
Copy code
name: CI/CD Pipeline

on:
  push:
    branches:
      - main

jobs:
  build:
    runs-on: ubuntu-latest
    steps:
      - name: Checkout code
        uses: actions/checkout@v2

      - name: Set up Node.js
        uses: actions/setup-node@v2
        with:
          node-version: '14'

      - name: Install dependencies
        run: npm install

      - name: Build Angular application
        run: ng build --prod

      - name: Publish ASP.NET Core application
        run: dotnet publish -c Release
```

1. **Deploy to Azure**: You can add steps to deploy your application to Azure directly within the workflow file.

Using Azure DevOps

1. **Create a New Pipeline**: In Azure DevOps, create a new pipeline for your repository.

2. **Select the Build Template**: Choose the ASP.NET Core template to build your API and add tasks for building your Angular application.
3. **Deploy to Azure**: Add deployment tasks to push the built artifacts to Azure App Service.

3. Testing in CI/CD

Integrate your tests in the CI/CD pipeline to ensure that code changes are validated before deployment. You can add testing steps in your workflow file for both Angular and ASP.NET Core.

```yaml
Copy code
- name: Run Angular tests
  run: npm test -- --watch=false

- name: Run .NET tests
  run: dotnet test
```

Securing Your Deployed Application

1. HTTPS Configuration

Always use HTTPS to encrypt data between the client and server. Most cloud providers automatically configure SSL for you, but ensure it is enabled in your application settings.

2. API Authentication

Ensure that your API endpoints are secured and require authentication using JWT tokens. This prevents unauthorized access to your resources.

3. CORS Configuration

Configure CORS policies to allow only trusted origins to access your API. This adds an additional layer of security to your application.

4. Regular Security Audits

Conduct regular security audits and vulnerability assessments of your deployed applications to identify and fix potential security risks.

Conclusion

In this chapter, you learned how to prepare your full-stack application for deployment, explore various hosting options for both ASP.NET Core and Angular applications, and implement CI/CD pipelines for automated deployments. You also gained insights into securing your deployed application to ensure it operates safely in production.

By following these deployment strategies, you can effectively launch your applications and make them accessible to users. In the next chapter, we will focus on performance optimization techniques for both Angular and ASP.NET Core to ensure your applications run smoothly and efficiently.

Chapter 10: Performance Optimization Techniques

Performance optimization is crucial in developing web applications to enhance user experience and ensure efficient resource utilization. This chapter covers various performance optimization techniques for both Angular front-end applications and ASP.NET Core back-end services. We will explore strategies that improve loading times, responsiveness, and overall efficiency.

1. Importance of Performance Optimization

1.1 User Experience

In today's digital landscape, users expect applications to be fast and responsive. Slow-loading applications can lead to frustration and abandonment, negatively impacting user experience and engagement.

1.2 SEO Benefits

For public-facing applications, performance plays a significant role in search engine optimization (SEO). Faster applications are favored by search engines, improving your site's visibility and ranking.

1.3 Resource Efficiency

Optimizing performance can lead to more efficient use of server resources and bandwidth, reducing operational costs and enhancing scalability.

1.4 Competitive Advantage

Applications that perform well can differentiate themselves from competitors, attracting more users and retaining existing ones.

2. Performance Optimization in Angular

2.1 Lazy Loading Modules

Lazy loading is a technique that allows you to load modules only when needed, significantly reducing the initial load time of your Angular application.

Implementing Lazy Loading

To implement lazy loading, define your feature modules with routing configurations that allow the Angular Router to load them on demand.

1. Create a new feature module:

```bash
Copy code
ng generate module feature --route feature --module app.module
```

1. In the app-routing.module.ts file, configure the lazy-loaded route:

```
typescript
Copy code
const routes: Routes = [
  { path: 'feature', loadChildren: () =>
  import('./feature/feature.module').then(m => m.FeatureModule) }
];
```

2.2 Ahead-of-Time (AOT) Compilation

AOT compilation compiles your application at build time rather than runtime, resulting in faster rendering and improved security.

Enabling AOT

AOT is enabled by default when you build your Angular application for production:

```
bash
Copy code
ng build --prod
```

2.3 Change Detection Strategy

Angular's default change detection strategy checks for changes in the entire component tree. By implementing the OnPush strategy, you can improve performance by reducing the number of checks.

Using OnPush Strategy

1. Modify your component:

```
typescript
Copy code
```

```
import { ChangeDetectionStrategy, Component } from
'@angular/core';

@Component({
  selector: 'app-my-component',
  templateUrl: './my-component.component.html',
  changeDetection: ChangeDetectionStrategy.OnPush
})
export class MyComponent {
  // Component logic
}
```

2.4 Optimize Template Expressions

Avoid complex expressions in your templates, as Angular evaluates them during change detection. Instead, compute values in the component and bind to those properties.

Example

Instead of:

```
html
Copy code
<p>{{ calculateValue() }}</p>
```

Use:

```
typescript
Copy code
public value = this.calculateValue();
```

Then bind to value in the template.

2.5 TrackBy Function in NgFor

Using ngFor with large lists can impact performance. Implementing a trackBy function helps Angular identify items in the list, optimizing rendering.

Example

```html
html
Copy code
<div *ngFor="let item of items; trackBy: trackById">
  {{ item.name }}
</div>
typescript
Copy code
trackById(index: number, item: Item): number {
  return item.id; // Unique identifier
}
```

2.6 Avoid Memory Leaks

Memory leaks can degrade performance over time. Unsubscribe from observables and detach event listeners in components to prevent leaks.

Example

In a component with subscriptions:

```typescript
typescript
Copy code
import { Subscription } from 'rxjs';

private subscriptions: Subscription = new Subscription();

ngOnInit(): void {
  const sub = this.myService.getData().subscribe();
  this.subscriptions.add(sub);
}
```

```
ngOnDestroy(): void {
  this.subscriptions.unsubscribe(); // Clean up
}
```

2.7 Optimize Image Loading

Images can significantly affect load times. Optimize images by using appropriate formats, compressing them, and implementing lazy loading.

Using Lazy Loading for Images

Use the loading="lazy" attribute for images to defer loading until they are in the viewport:

```html
Copy code
<img src="image.jpg" loading="lazy" alt="Description">
```

3. Performance Optimization in ASP.NET Core

3.1 Use Asynchronous Programming

ASP.NET Core supports asynchronous programming to improve the scalability and responsiveness of your applications. Use async and await keywords for I/O-bound operations, such as database calls or API requests.

Implementing Async Actions

Modify your controller actions to be asynchronous:

```csharp
Copy code
[HttpGet]
public async Task<ActionResult<IEnumerable<Product>>>
```

```
GetProducts()
{
    var products = await _context.Products.ToListAsync();
    return Ok(products);
}
```

3.2 Caching Strategies

Implement caching to reduce database load and improve response times. ASP.NET Core supports in-memory caching, distributed caching, and response caching.

Using In-Memory Caching

1. Register caching services in Startup.cs:

```csharp
Copy code
public void ConfigureServices(IServiceCollection services)
{
    services.AddMemoryCache();
    // Other services...
}
```

1. Use caching in your controller:

```csharp
Copy code
private readonly IMemoryCache _cache;

public ProductsController(ApplicationDbContext context,
```

```
IMemoryCache cache)
{
    _context = context;
    _cache = cache;
}


[HttpGet]
public async Task<ActionResult<IEnumerable<Product>>>
GetProducts()
{
    if (!_cache.TryGetValue("products", out List<Product>
    products))
    {
        products = await _context.Products.ToListAsync();
        _cache.Set("products", products,
        TimeSpan.FromMinutes(5)); // Cache for 5 minutes
    }

    return Ok(products);
}
```

3.3 Optimize Database Queries

Efficient database queries can significantly impact application performance.
Use **Entity Framework Core** features like Include, Select, and pagination
to optimize queries.

Example: Using Include for Related Data

When retrieving data with related entities, use Include to avoid N+1 query
problems:

```
csharp
Copy code
var products = await _context.Products.Include(p =>
p.Category).ToListAsync();
```

3.4 Connection Pooling

ASP.NET Core automatically uses connection pooling when using database providers like SQL Server. Ensure that your connection strings are configured correctly to take advantage of this feature.

3.5 Gzip Compression

Enabling Gzip compression reduces the size of the response body, leading to faster transfer times. You can enable Gzip in your ASP.NET Core application by adding middleware.

1. Install the Microsoft.AspNetCore.ResponseCompression package:

```bash
Copy code
dotnet add package Microsoft.AspNetCore.ResponseCompression
```

1. Update Startup.cs to configure compression:

```csharp
Copy code
public void ConfigureServices(IServiceCollection services)
{
    services.AddResponseCompression(options =>
    {
        options.EnableForHttps = true; // Enable for HTTPS
    });
}
```

1. Add the middleware in the Configure method:

```csharp
Copy code
public void Configure(IApplicationBuilder app,
IWebHostEnvironment env)
{
    app.UseResponseCompression();
    // Other middleware...
}
```

4. Advanced Performance Monitoring

4.1 Use Application Performance Monitoring (APM)

Integrating APM tools can help you identify performance bottlenecks in your application. Tools like **New Relic**, **Dynatrace**, or **Application Insights** can provide insights into your application's performance, dependencies, and usage patterns.

4.2 Logging and Diagnostics

ASP.NET Core includes built-in logging support that can help you diagnose issues and monitor performance. Use the logging framework to capture performance metrics and error information.

Example of Logging

```csharp
Copy code
public class ProductsController : ControllerBase
{
    private readonly ILogger<ProductsController> _logger;

    public ProductsController(ILogger<ProductsController> logger)
```

```
    {
        _logger = logger;
    }

    [HttpGet]
    public async Task<ActionResult<IEnumerable<Product>>>
    GetProducts()
    {
        _logger.LogInformation("Fetching products...");
        var products = await _context.Products.ToListAsync();
        return Ok(products);
    }
}
```

4.3 Profiling Tools

Use profiling tools to analyze application performance. Tools like **MiniPro-filer** or **dotTrace** can help identify slow database queries, memory usage, and CPU utilization.

5. Client-Side Performance Optimization Techniques

5.1 Reduce Bundle Size

Minimize the size of your Angular application by optimizing the bundle. Use the Angular CLI to perform the following:

1. **Tree Shaking**: This removes unused code during the build process. Ensure your build configuration is set to production mode:

```bash
Copy code
```

```
ng build --prod
```

1. **Code Splitting**: Use lazy loading to create smaller bundles that load only when needed.

5.2 Optimize Third-Party Libraries

Be mindful of the third-party libraries you include in your Angular application. Large libraries can significantly increase bundle size. Use alternatives or load libraries conditionally to keep your application lightweight.

5.3 Image Optimization

Images can often take up a significant portion of your application's size. Use tools like **ImageMagick** or **TinyPNG** to compress and optimize images before deployment.

5.4 Use CDNs for Static Assets

Using Content Delivery Networks (CDNs) for serving static assets like images, CSS, and JavaScript files can greatly improve load times by distributing content closer to users geographically.

5.5 Lazy Loading for Images

Implement lazy loading for images to defer loading until they are visible in the viewport. Use the loading="lazy" attribute for images:

```html
Copy code
<img src="image.jpg" loading="lazy" alt="Description">
```

6. Server-Side Performance Optimization Techniques

6.1 Optimize Database Performance

Database performance can often be a bottleneck in web applications. Optimize your database by:

1. **Indexing**: Ensure that your database tables are properly indexed to speed up query performance.
2. **Query Optimization**: Analyze your SQL queries and refactor them for better performance.
3. **Database Scaling**: Consider horizontal or vertical scaling strategies to accommodate increased load.

6.2 Configure Connection String Options

Optimize your connection string settings to ensure efficient database connectivity. Consider settings for connection pooling, command timeouts, and other performance-related options.

6.3 Implement Rate Limiting

Rate limiting helps to control the number of requests a user can make in a given period. This can protect your server from excessive requests and enhance overall performance.

Implementing Rate Limiting in ASP.NET Core

You can use middleware to implement rate limiting in your API:

1. Install the AspNetCoreRateLimit package:

```bash
Copy code
dotnet add package AspNetCoreRateLimit
```

1. Configure rate limiting in Startup.cs:

```csharp
Copy code
public void ConfigureServices(IServiceCollection services)
{
    services.AddMemoryCache();
    services.Configure<IpRateLimitOptions>(options =>
    {
        options.GeneralRules = new List<RateLimitPolicy>
        {
            new RateLimitPolicy
            {
                Endpoint = "*",
                Limit = 100,
                Period = "1h"
            }
        };
    });

    services.AddInMemoryRateLimiting();
    services.AddSingleton<IRateLimitConfiguration,
    RateLimitConfiguration>();
}
```

1. Add the middleware in the Configure method:

```csharp
csharp
Copy code
public void Configure(IApplicationBuilder app,
IWebHostEnvironment env)
{
    app.UseIpRateLimiting();
    // Other middleware...
}
```

Conclusion

In this chapter, we explored various performance optimization techniques for both Angular and ASP.NET Core applications. We discussed strategies for lazy loading, AOT compilation, caching, reducing bundle sizes, and optimizing database performance.

By implementing these techniques, you can significantly improve the speed, responsiveness, and overall user experience of your full-stack application. In the next chapter, we will focus on best practices for maintaining and updating your application post-deployment, ensuring it continues to perform well and meets user needs.

Chapter 11: Best Practices for Application Maintenance and Updates

Maintaining and updating a web application after deployment is essential to ensure it continues to perform well, meets user expectations, and remains secure. In this chapter, we will explore best practices for maintaining and updating your full-stack application, focusing on aspects such as monitoring, bug fixing, updating dependencies, enhancing features, and ensuring security.

1. The Importance of Maintenance

1.1 Performance Optimization

Regular maintenance allows you to identify and address performance issues that may arise as your application scales and user behavior changes. This helps keep response times fast and resource utilization efficient.

1.2 Security

Cybersecurity threats are constantly evolving. Regularly updating your application and its dependencies helps protect against vulnerabilities that could be exploited by attackers.

1.3 User Experience

User expectations evolve over time. Maintaining your application allows you to respond to user feedback, improve usability, and add new features that enhance the overall user experience.

1.4 Compliance

Many industries have regulations regarding data protection and privacy. Regular maintenance ensures your application remains compliant with applicable laws and standards.

2. Monitoring Your Application

2.1 Setting Up Application Performance Monitoring (APM)

APM tools help you monitor the performance of your application in real time. These tools provide insights into response times, error rates, and resource usage, enabling you to identify and address issues quickly.

Popular APM Tools

- **New Relic**: Provides detailed insights into application performance, including slow transactions and error tracking.
- **Application Insights**: A part of Azure Monitor, it offers APM capabilities for .NET applications, tracking requests, exceptions, and custom events.
- **Dynatrace**: Offers comprehensive monitoring for applications, infrastructure, and user experience.

2.2 Setting Up Logging

Implementing a robust logging strategy is crucial for diagnosing issues and understanding application behavior.

Best Practices for Logging

- **Log Levels**: Use different log levels (e.g., Debug, Info, Warning, Error, Fatal) to categorize log messages. This helps filter out noise and focus on critical issues.
- **Structured Logging**: Use structured logging formats (like JSON) to make log data easier to query and analyze.
- **Centralized Logging**: Use tools like **ELK Stack (Elasticsearch, Logstash, Kibana)** or **Splunk** to aggregate logs from multiple services into a centralized location for easier access and analysis.

2.3 User Feedback and Analytics

Incorporate user feedback mechanisms within your application to gather insights directly from users. Combine this with analytics tools (like Google Analytics) to track user interactions, behavior patterns, and popular features.

Implementing User Feedback

- **Surveys**: Periodically prompt users to provide feedback about their experience.
- **Feature Requests**: Allow users to suggest new features or improvements directly within the application.

3. Bug Fixing and Issue Tracking

3.1 Establishing a Bug Tracking System

A bug tracking system is essential for managing reported issues and monitoring their resolution.

Popular Bug Tracking Tools

- **Jira**: A widely used project management tool that includes issue tracking features.
- **Trello**: A flexible board-based tool that can be adapted for bug tracking.
- **GitHub Issues**: Integrated directly with your code repository, making it easy to track issues alongside code changes.

3.2 Prioritizing Bugs

Not all bugs are equal. Establish a system for prioritizing issues based on their severity and impact on users. Common classifications include:

- **Critical**: Application crashes or data loss.
- **Major**: Significant functionality is impaired.
- **Minor**: Cosmetic issues or non-critical bugs.

3.3 Regular Bug Fixes

Establish a routine for addressing reported issues. Regularly allocate time in your development cycle to fix bugs, ensuring that you maintain a healthy application.

4. Updating Dependencies

4.1 Keeping Dependencies Up to Date

Regularly update the libraries and frameworks your application depends on. This is crucial for ensuring compatibility, performance, and security.

Tools for Managing Dependencies

- **npm-check-updates**: A command-line tool that allows you to easily upgrade your package.json dependencies.
- **Dependabot**: An automated tool integrated with GitHub that automatically opens pull requests to update dependencies.

4.2 Testing After Updates

Before deploying updates, always run your application's test suite to ensure that updates to dependencies have not introduced any breaking changes.

Integration Tests

Make sure your integration tests cover critical paths in your application to verify that new dependencies do not affect functionality.

4.3 Handling Breaking Changes

When updating dependencies, review the changelog for breaking changes. If a library introduces breaking changes, you may need to refactor your code to accommodate the updates.

5. Enhancing Features and User Experience

5.1 Iterative Development

Adopt an iterative development approach, where you continuously refine and enhance your application based on user feedback and analytics. This allows you to adapt quickly to changing user needs.

5.2 Feature Flags

Implement feature flags to manage new features in production without deploying new code. This allows you to test features with a subset of users before a full rollout.

Using Feature Flags

1. **Configuration**: Use configuration files or databases to manage feature flags.
2. **Implementation**: Wrap new features in conditionals that check the status of the feature flag.

```typescript
Copy code
if (featureFlags.newFeatureEnabled) {
  // Implement new feature
}
```

5.3 Regular User Testing

Conduct regular user testing sessions to observe how users interact with your application. Gather feedback on usability and identify areas for improvement.

Methods for User Testing

- **A/B Testing**: Compare two versions of a feature to determine which performs better.
- **Usability Testing**: Observe users as they interact with your application to identify pain points.

6. Security Updates and Best Practices

6.1 Regular Security Audits

Conduct regular security audits of your application to identify vulnerabilities. Use automated tools and manual reviews to ensure compliance with best security practices.

Popular Security Tools

- **OWASP ZAP**: A free, open-source web application security scanner.
- **SonarQube**: A tool for continuous inspection of code quality and security vulnerabilities.

6.2 Updating Security Libraries

Ensure that any libraries related to security (such as authentication and encryption libraries) are kept up to date. Vulnerabilities in outdated libraries can expose your application to attacks.

6.3 Implementing Secure Coding Practices

Train your development team in secure coding practices, including:

- **Input Validation**: Always validate and sanitize user input to prevent injection attacks.
- **Error Handling**: Avoid revealing sensitive information in error messages. Use generic messages instead.

6.4 Monitor Security Vulnerabilities

Stay informed about security vulnerabilities that may affect your application. Subscribe to security mailing lists or use tools like **Snyk** to monitor dependencies for known vulnerabilities.

7. Documentation and Knowledge Sharing

7.1 Keeping Documentation Updated

Maintain up-to-date documentation for your application, including installation instructions, API documentation, and user guides. Well-documented applications are easier to maintain and enhance.

Documentation Tools

- **Swagger**: For generating API documentation automatically.
- **Markdown**: Use Markdown files for creating user guides and technical documentation.

7.2 Knowledge Sharing Within the Team

Encourage knowledge sharing among team members through:

- **Code Reviews**: Regular code reviews help spread knowledge of the codebase.
- **Pair Programming**: Working together can help team members learn from one another.

7.3 Conducting Regular Team Meetings

Hold regular meetings to discuss ongoing maintenance tasks, bugs, feature enhancements, and security issues. This promotes collaboration and keeps everyone informed.

8. Preparing for Future Scalability

8.1 Scalability Considerations

As your application grows, it's essential to ensure that it can handle increased load and user activity. Plan for scalability in both your architecture and code.
Vertical vs. Horizontal Scaling

- **Vertical Scaling**: Increasing the resources (CPU, RAM) of a single server.
- **Horizontal Scaling**: Adding more servers to distribute the load.

8.2 Use Microservices Architecture

Consider breaking down your application into microservices. This approach allows you to scale individual components independently and improve maintainability.

8.3 Database Optimization

Optimize your database for scalability by:

- **Sharding**: Distributing data across multiple databases.
- **Replication**: Creating copies of the database to improve read performance.

8.4 Load Testing

Conduct load testing to simulate user traffic and evaluate how your application performs under stress. Tools like **Apache JMeter** or **Gatling** can help assess the application's scalability.

9. Continuous Improvement and Evolution

9.1 Stay Updated with Technology Trends

Technology is continually evolving, and so should your application. Stay updated with the latest trends and best practices in web development, security, and user experience.

9.2 Gather User Feedback Regularly

Establish mechanisms for regularly collecting user feedback and analyzing user behavior. Use this information to prioritize features and improvements.

9.3 Iterate on Features

Adopt an iterative approach to feature development, regularly releasing updates and enhancements based on user feedback and testing results.

9.4 Conduct Post-Mortem Reviews

After significant incidents (like outages or security breaches), conduct post-mortem reviews to analyze what went wrong, identify lessons learned, and develop action plans to prevent future issues.

Conclusion

In this chapter, we explored best practices for maintaining and updating your full-stack application post-deployment. We covered the importance of monitoring, bug fixing, updating dependencies, enhancing features, and ensuring security.

By implementing these practices, you can ensure your application remains performant, secure, and aligned with user needs over time. In the next chapter, we will summarize the key concepts covered throughout the book and provide final thoughts on building and maintaining successful full-stack applications.

Chapter 12: Conclusion and Key Takeaways

As we reach the conclusion of this book, it's essential to reflect on the journey of building a full-stack application using Angular and ASP.NET Core. This chapter summarizes the key concepts covered throughout the book, emphasizes best practices, and provides final thoughts on successfully developing and maintaining modern web applications.

1. Recap of Key Concepts

1.1 Full-Stack Development Overview

Full-stack development encompasses both front-end and back-end development, allowing developers to create complete web applications. Throughout this book, we explored how to leverage Angular for the front end and ASP.NET Core for the back end, providing a robust foundation for building dynamic applications.

1.2 Angular Framework Essentials

We discussed the Angular framework's architecture, including its component-based structure, module system, and dependency injection. Key topics included:

- **Components**: Building blocks of Angular applications that encapsulate templates and logic.
- **Services**: Classes that provide shared functionality, promoting code reuse and separation of concerns.
- **Routing**: Managing navigation and state within single-page applications.
- **Forms**: Handling user input and validation through reactive and template-driven forms.

1.3 ASP.NET Core Fundamentals

On the back end, we delved into ASP.NET Core, covering essential topics such as:

- **Web APIs**: Building RESTful services that can be consumed by various clients.
- **Entity Framework Core**: Interacting with databases using an ORM to simplify data access and manipulation.
- **Authentication and Authorization**: Securing applications using JWT tokens and implementing role-based access control.
- **Testing**: Ensuring application quality through unit tests, integration tests, and end-to-end testing.

1.4 Deployment Strategies

We explored various deployment options, including cloud platforms such as Azure and AWS, as well as static site hosting solutions for Angular applications. Key points included:

- **Building and preparing applications** for production.
- **Hosting**: Choosing the right environment for deploying applications, whether through PaaS solutions or self-hosting.
- **CI/CD**: Implementing continuous integration and deployment pipelines to automate testing and deployment processes.

1.5 Performance Optimization Techniques

To enhance application performance, we covered numerous optimization techniques for both Angular and ASP.NET Core, including:

- **Lazy Loading**: Reducing initial load times by loading modules on demand.
- **AOT Compilation**: Compiling Angular applications before deployment for improved speed.
- **Caching**: Utilizing in-memory caching and response caching in ASP.NET Core.
- **Database Optimization**: Improving query performance and database scaling strategies.

1.6 Maintenance and Updates

Maintaining and updating your application post-deployment is crucial for long-term success. We discussed:

- **Monitoring**: Setting up application performance monitoring (APM) and logging to track application health.

- **Bug Tracking**: Implementing systems for tracking and prioritizing issues.
- **Dependency Management**: Regularly updating libraries and frameworks to ensure security and compatibility.
- **User Feedback**: Iteratively improving your application based on user feedback and analytics.

2. Best Practices for Building Full-Stack Applications

2.1 Prioritize User Experience

User experience should be at the forefront of your development process. Focus on:

- **Responsive Design**: Ensure your application works seamlessly across various devices and screen sizes.
- **Accessibility**: Implement features that make your application usable for people with disabilities.
- **Performance**: Continuously optimize loading times and responsiveness.

2.2 Embrace Agile Development

Adopting Agile methodologies can enhance your development process by promoting flexibility, collaboration, and iterative improvements. Key practices include:

- **Regular Stand-Ups**: Keep the team aligned with daily or weekly meetings to discuss progress and blockers.
- **Sprint Planning**: Organize development into short, manageable sprints focused on delivering specific features.

2.3 Foster Collaboration and Communication

Encouraging collaboration among team members is vital for success. Use tools like:

- **Version Control**: Git for managing code changes and facilitating collaboration.
- **Documentation**: Maintain up-to-date documentation to ensure all team members have access to essential information.

2.4 Invest in Testing

Building a comprehensive testing strategy is essential for maintaining code quality. Consider:

- **Automated Testing**: Implement unit tests, integration tests, and end-to-end tests to catch issues early in the development process.
- **Test Coverage**: Monitor test coverage to ensure critical paths in your application are adequately tested.

2.5 Focus on Security

Security should be a priority from the start. Implement best practices such as:

- **Input Validation**: Always validate and sanitize user input to prevent injection attacks.
- **Regular Security Audits**: Conduct periodic security assessments to identify and address vulnerabilities.

3. Future Trends in Full-Stack Development

3.1 Serverless Architectures

Serverless architectures are gaining popularity, allowing developers to build applications without managing server infrastructure. With platforms like AWS Lambda and Azure Functions, developers can focus on writing code while automatically scaling based on demand.

3.2 Microservices and Containerization

Microservices architecture allows applications to be broken down into smaller, independent services. Containerization technologies like Docker facilitate deploying and managing these services, promoting scalability and isolation.

3.3 Progressive Web Applications (PWAs)

PWAs combine the best features of web and mobile applications, providing offline capabilities, push notifications, and improved performance. They enhance user engagement and can be installed on devices like native apps.

3.4 Artificial Intelligence and Machine Learning

Integrating AI and machine learning into applications can enhance user experiences through personalized recommendations, chatbots, and data analytics. As these technologies become more accessible, developers should consider how to incorporate them into their applications.

3.5 Continued Focus on Performance and Security

As applications grow in complexity, the need for performance optimization and security will only increase. Developers should stay informed about best practices and emerging technologies to ensure their applications remain competitive.

4. Final Thoughts

Building and maintaining a full-stack application using Angular and ASP.NET Core requires a solid understanding of both front-end and back-end technologies, as well as best practices in development, deployment, and maintenance. Throughout this book, we have explored the essential concepts and techniques that contribute to the success of a modern web application.

By prioritizing user experience, adopting agile methodologies, fostering collaboration, investing in testing, and focusing on security, you can create applications that not only meet user expectations but also thrive in a rapidly changing technological landscape.

Remember that the journey of development is ongoing. Stay curious, keep learning, and adapt to new trends and challenges as they arise. With the knowledge and skills gained from this book, you are well-equipped to embark on your journey as a full-stack developer and make meaningful contributions to the world of web development.

Chapter 13: Real-World Applications and Case Studies

I
n this chapter, we will explore real-world applications built with Angular and ASP.NET Core, examining how these technologies are applied to solve complex problems. We will discuss various case studies across different industries, illustrating the versatility and effectiveness of this tech stack. By analyzing these examples, you will gain insights into best practices, design patterns, and the practical implications of building robust, scalable applications.

1. Overview of Case Studies

Case studies provide valuable insights into how different organizations have successfully implemented full-stack applications. We will cover applications in various sectors, including:

1. E-commerce
2. Healthcare
3. Education
4. Social Media
5. Finance

Each section will detail the challenges faced, the solutions implemented, and the technologies used, highlighting the impact on the organization's overall performance and user experience.

2. Case Study 1: E-Commerce Application

2.1 Background

An e-commerce company, **ShopSmart**, sought to enhance its online shopping experience by building a new web application. The goal was to create a platform that would allow users to browse products, manage their carts, and complete purchases seamlessly. The existing application suffered from performance issues and lacked modern features.

2.2 Challenges Faced

- **Slow Performance**: The existing application had long loading times, especially during peak traffic periods.
- **User Experience**: Users reported difficulties in navigating the platform, leading to high cart abandonment rates.
- **Mobile Responsiveness**: The previous application was not mobile-friendly, limiting access for users on smartphones and tablets.

2.3 Solutions Implemented

Technology Stack

- **Front-End**: Angular was chosen for its component-based architecture and powerful features for building dynamic user interfaces.
- **Back-End**: ASP.NET Core was utilized for its performance and scalability, enabling efficient handling of API requests.
- **Database**: SQL Server was used for data storage, with Entity Framework Core facilitating data access.

Key Features Developed

1. **Dynamic Product Catalog**: The new application featured a dynamic product catalog, allowing users to filter and search for products easily.
2. **Real-Time Inventory Management**: Integration with a back-end inventory system ensured users could see real-time stock availability.
3. **Mobile Optimization**: The application was designed to be fully responsive, providing an optimal experience on all devices.

Performance Optimization

- **Lazy Loading**: Modules were implemented with lazy loading to reduce initial load times.
- **AOT Compilation**: The application was built using Ahead-of-Time compilation for faster rendering.
- **Caching**: Server-side caching was implemented to speed up data retrieval for frequently accessed products.

2.4 Results Achieved

- **Performance Improvement**: The new application experienced a 60% reduction in load times, significantly enhancing user experience.
- **Increased Sales**: User engagement increased by 30%, leading to a substantial rise in conversion rates and sales.
- **Mobile Access**: The responsive design resulted in a 40% increase in mobile users accessing the platform.

2.5 Lessons Learned

The implementation of the ShopSmart application highlighted the importance of performance optimization, user-centric design, and the effective use of modern frameworks in enhancing e-commerce experiences.

3. Case Study 2: Healthcare Management System

3.1 Background

HealthTrack, a healthcare provider, aimed to develop a comprehensive management system for patient records, appointments, and billing. The goal was to streamline operations, improve patient care, and ensure compliance with healthcare regulations.

3.2 Challenges Faced

- **Fragmented Systems**: HealthTrack struggled with multiple disconnected systems, leading to inefficiencies and data inconsistencies.
- **Patient Accessibility**: Patients had difficulty accessing their records and managing appointments online.
- **Regulatory Compliance**: The existing systems were not compliant with healthcare regulations, posing risks for data security.

3.3 Solutions Implemented

Technology Stack

- **Front-End**: Angular was selected for building a user-friendly interface that allows healthcare professionals and patients to access information easily.
- **Back-End**: ASP.NET Core was chosen for its security features, ensuring sensitive health information was protected.
- **Database**: SQL Server was used to store patient records, appointment schedules, and billing information.

Key Features Developed

1. **Patient Portal**: A secure patient portal was created, allowing patients

to view their records, request appointments, and communicate with healthcare providers.

2. **Appointment Scheduling**: The application included a robust scheduling system that enabled both patients and staff to manage appointments effectively.

3. **Billing System**: An integrated billing system streamlined billing processes, reducing errors and improving payment collection.

Security Measures

- **Role-Based Access Control**: Implemented to restrict access to sensitive information based on user roles (doctors, nurses, patients).
- **Data Encryption**: Sensitive data was encrypted both in transit and at rest, ensuring compliance with healthcare regulations (HIPAA).

3.4 Results Achieved

- **Operational Efficiency**: The integrated system improved operational efficiency by 50%, reducing administrative burdens on staff.
- **Enhanced Patient Experience**: Patient satisfaction ratings increased significantly due to improved access to information and services.
- **Regulatory Compliance**: The new system ensured compliance with healthcare regulations, reducing the risk of legal issues.

3.5 Lessons Learned

The HealthTrack case study underscores the importance of data security, regulatory compliance, and the benefits of a centralized system for managing complex operations in the healthcare industry.

4. Case Study 3: Online Learning Platform

4.1 Background

EduHub is an online learning platform aimed at providing quality educational resources to students globally. The organization wanted to create a modern web application that offered interactive courses, assessments, and community features.

4.2 Challenges Faced

- **User Engagement**: The existing platform had low user engagement and retention rates.
- **Content Management**: Course management was cumbersome, making it difficult to update and deliver new content.
- **Performance Issues**: The application experienced slow loading times, particularly during high traffic periods.

4.3 Solutions Implemented

Technology Stack

- **Front-End**: Angular was chosen for its ability to create dynamic user interfaces with rich interactivity.
- **Back-End**: ASP.NET Core was used to build RESTful APIs that support course content delivery and user management.
- **Database**: A NoSQL database (MongoDB) was used to manage diverse content types, allowing for flexibility in course structure.

Key Features Developed

1. **Interactive Course Modules**: The platform featured interactive modules that included videos, quizzes, and discussion forums.
2. **Real-Time Collaboration**: Implemented features that allowed students to collaborate in real time, enhancing community engagement.

3. **Admin Dashboard**: A user-friendly admin dashboard was created for content creators to easily manage courses, track progress, and analyze user engagement.

Performance Optimization

- **Content Delivery Network (CDN)**: Used for serving static assets like images and videos, improving load times.
- **Progressive Web App (PWA)**: The application was developed as a PWA, allowing offline access and improving performance on mobile devices.

4.4 Results Achieved

- **Increased User Engagement**: The new platform saw a 70% increase in user engagement, with higher course completion rates.
- **Scalability**: The flexible architecture allowed EduHub to easily scale and add new features as needed.
- **Positive User Feedback**: User satisfaction surveys indicated a significant improvement in the learning experience.

4.5 Lessons Learned

The EduHub case study highlights the importance of user engagement, the benefits of interactive content, and the role of technology in creating a flexible and scalable learning environment.

5. Case Study 4: Social Media Application

5.1 Background

ConnectMe is a social media application designed to facilitate communication and connections among users. The platform aimed to create a space for sharing content, networking, and building communities.

5.2 Challenges Faced

- **Scalability Issues**: The existing infrastructure struggled to handle rapid user growth and increased activity.
- **Performance Bottlenecks**: Users experienced slow loading times, particularly with multimedia content.
- **User Retention**: The platform faced challenges in retaining users due to limited engagement features.

5.3 Solutions Implemented

Technology Stack

- **Front-End**: Angular was utilized for its capability to create a responsive and dynamic user interface.
- **Back-End**: ASP.NET Core was chosen for its scalability and performance, with SignalR used for real-time communication.
- **Database**: A combination of SQL Server for structured data and Redis for caching was implemented to enhance performance.

Key Features Developed

1. **Real-Time Messaging**: Integrated SignalR to enable real-time messaging and notifications among users.
2. **Feed Algorithm**: Developed a custom feed algorithm to prioritize user engagement and relevant content.
3. **Multimedia Sharing**: Optimized the platform for multimedia content sharing, allowing users to post images, videos, and links seamlessly.

Performance Optimization

- **Content Caching**: Implemented caching strategies to store frequently accessed content, reducing load times.

- **Database Indexing**: Used indexing to speed up database queries related to user interactions and content retrieval.

5.4 Results Achieved

- **User Growth**: The platform experienced a 150% increase in user registrations within the first few months after launch.
- **Improved Engagement**: Real-time features significantly improved user engagement, leading to longer session durations and increased interaction.
- **Positive Community Feedback**: Users reported higher satisfaction levels due to enhanced features and performance.

5.5 Lessons Learned

The ConnectMe case study emphasizes the importance of scalability, real-time features, and user engagement in creating a successful social media application.

6. Case Study 5: Financial Management Application

6.1 Background

FinancePro is a financial management application aimed at helping users track expenses, create budgets, and manage investments. The organization sought to build a comprehensive web application that provides users with insights into their financial health.

6.2 Challenges Faced

- **Data Security**: The application needed to ensure the highest level of security to protect sensitive financial information.
- **Integration with Third-Party APIs**: The need to integrate with vari-

ous financial data sources and APIs posed challenges in data consistency and management.

- **User Experience**: Users reported difficulties in navigating the application and understanding financial insights.

6.3 Solutions Implemented

Technology Stack

- **Front-End**: Angular was chosen for its ability to create dynamic and interactive data visualizations.
- **Back-End**: ASP.NET Core was selected for its security features and ability to integrate with external APIs.
- **Database**: SQL Server was used for data storage, with encryption to protect sensitive information.

Key Features Developed

1. **Dashboard**: A customizable dashboard provided users with insights into their financial health through graphs, charts, and notifications.
2. **Budgeting Tools**: Users could set budgets and track expenses against their goals, with automatic alerts for overspending.
3. **API Integrations**: Integrated with various financial data providers to give users real-time updates on their investments and accounts.

Security Measures

- **Data Encryption**: Used AES encryption for sensitive financial data, ensuring compliance with financial regulations.
- **Two-Factor Authentication (2FA)**: Implemented 2FA to enhance account security for users.

6.4 Results Achieved

- **Increased User Trust**: Enhanced security measures led to increased user trust and satisfaction, as users felt secure managing their finances online.
- **Higher Engagement**: The interactive dashboard and budgeting tools improved user engagement, resulting in a 40% increase in active users.
- **Seamless Data Integration**: Successful integration with third-party APIs allowed users to have a comprehensive view of their financial data in one place.

6.5 Lessons Learned

The FinancePro case study illustrates the importance of security, user experience, and effective data integration in building a financial management application.

7. Key Takeaways from the Case Studies

7.1 Importance of Choosing the Right Tech Stack

Selecting the appropriate technology stack is critical to the success of any application. Angular and ASP.NET Core provide a powerful combination for building robust and scalable applications across various industries.

7.2 User-Centric Design is Crucial

Designing applications with the user in mind is vital. Prioritizing user experience, accessibility, and engagement features can significantly impact the adoption and retention of the application.

7.3 Performance Optimization Should Be Ongoing

Performance should be a continuous focus throughout the application lifecycle. Regular optimization, monitoring, and adaptation to user feedback will ensure the application remains responsive and efficient.

7.4 Security is Non-Negotiable

In an era of increasing cybersecurity threats, prioritizing security measures is essential. Implementing best practices for data protection, authentication, and access control is necessary to build user trust.

7.5 Adaptability and Scalability Are Key

Applications must be designed to adapt to changing user needs and technological advancements. Scalability is crucial for accommodating growth and ensuring long-term viability.

8. Final Thoughts

The journey of building full-stack applications using Angular and ASP.NET Core is both challenging and rewarding. By analyzing real-world case studies, we gain valuable insights into the practical application of concepts discussed throughout this book.

As you embark on your development journey, remember that continuous learning, adaptation, and user feedback are essential components of successful application development. Embrace new technologies and methodologies, stay informed about industry trends, and always prioritize the user experience.

Chapter 14: Advanced Topics and Future Trends in Full-Stack Development

As the landscape of web development evolves, new challenges and opportunities arise. This chapter delves into advanced topics in full-stack development, explores emerging trends, and discusses how developers can prepare for future developments in the field. We will cover:

1. Advanced State Management in Angular
2. Progressive Web Applications (PWAs)
3. Microservices Architecture
4. Serverless Computing
5. API-First Development
6. Continuous Integration and Continuous Deployment (CI/CD)
7. The Future of Web Development

By the end of this chapter, you will have a deeper understanding of advanced concepts and be equipped to embrace future trends in full-stack development.

1. Advanced State Management in Angular

1.1 Understanding State Management

State management refers to how you manage the data (state) of your application. In complex applications, especially those with multiple components that share data, managing state can become challenging. Proper state management ensures that the application's data is consistent and easily accessible throughout different components.

1.2 Using NgRx for State Management

NgRx is a popular state management library for Angular applications, inspired by Redux. It uses a unidirectional data flow and centralizes the application state in a store.

Core Concepts of NgRx

1. **Store**: A single source of truth that holds the application state.
2. **Actions**: Events that trigger state changes. Actions are plain objects that have a type and optional payload.
3. **Reducers**: Pure functions that specify how the state changes in response to actions.
4. **Selectors**: Functions that select pieces of state from the store.

Setting Up NgRx

1. **Install NgRx:**

```bash
Copy code
ng add @ngrx/store
ng add @ngrx/effects
```

```
ng add @ngrx/store-devtools
```

1. **Create Actions**:

```typescript
typescript
Copy code
import { createAction, props } from '@ngrx/store';

export const loadProducts = createAction('[Product List] Load
Products');
export const loadProductsSuccess = createAction(
  '[Product List] Load Products Success',
  props<{ products: Product[] }>()
);
export const loadProductsFailure = createAction(
  '[Product List] Load Products Failure',
  props<{ error: string }>()
);
```

1. **Create Reducers**:

```typescript
typescript
Copy code
import { createReducer, on } from '@ngrx/store';
import { loadProducts, loadProductsSuccess, loadProductsFailure }
from './product.actions';

export interface ProductState {
  products: Product[];
  loading: boolean;
  error: string;
}

export const initialState: ProductState = {
```

```
  products: [],
  loading: false,
  error: ''
};

export const productReducer = createReducer(
  initialState,
  on(loadProducts, state => ({ ...state, loading: true })),
  on(loadProductsSuccess, (state, { products }) => ({ ...state,
  loading: false, products })),
  on(loadProductsFailure, (state, { error }) => ({ ...state,
  loading: false, error }))
);
```

1. **Create Effects**:

Effects allow you to handle side effects, such as API calls:

```typescript
Copy code
import { Injectable } from '@angular/core';
import { Actions, createEffect, ofType } from '@ngrx/effects';
import { ProductService } from './product.service';
import { loadProducts, loadProductsSuccess, loadProductsFailure }
from './product.actions';
import { catchError, map, mergeMap } from 'rxjs/operators';

@Injectable()
export class ProductEffects {
  constructor(
    private actions$: Actions,
    private productService: ProductService
  ) {}

  loadProducts$ = createEffect(() =>
    this.actions$.pipe(
      ofType(loadProducts),
```

```
    mergeMap(() =>
      this.productService.getProducts().pipe(
        map(products => loadProductsSuccess({ products })),
        catchError(error => loadProductsFailure({ error }))
      )
    )
  )
);
}
```

1. **Using the Store in Components**:

```typescript
Copy code
import { Store } from '@ngrx/store';
import { loadProducts } from './product.actions';

@Component({
  // component metadata
})
export class ProductListComponent implements OnInit {
  products$ = this.store.select(selectAllProducts);

  constructor(private store: Store) {}

  ngOnInit() {
    this.store.dispatch(loadProducts());
  }
}
```

1.3 Benefits of NgRx

- **Predictable State Management**: A centralized store and strict rules for data flow make state changes predictable.
- **Debugging Capabilities**: NgRx DevTools allow you to inspect state changes and actions in real time.
- **Enhanced Maintainability**: The structure of actions, reducers, and effects promotes a clear separation of concerns.

2. Progressive Web Applications (PWAs)

2.1 What is a PWA?

Progressive Web Applications (PWAs) are web applications that use modern web capabilities to deliver an app-like experience to users. PWAs offer features such as offline access, push notifications, and installation on devices, improving user engagement and retention.

2.2 Key Features of PWAs

1. **Offline Support**: PWAs use service workers to cache assets and data, allowing them to work offline or on poor network connections.
2. **Responsive Design**: PWAs adapt to different screen sizes, providing a seamless experience across devices.
3. **App-Like Experience**: Users can install PWAs on their devices, making them feel like native applications.

2.3 Building a PWA with Angular

To convert an Angular application into a PWA:

1. **Add PWA Support**:

```bash
bash
Copy code
ng add @angular/pwa
```

This command adds a service worker and necessary configuration to your Angular project.

1. **Configure the Service Worker**: Modify the ngsw-config.json file to specify how caching should work:

```json
json
Copy code
{
  "index": "/index.html",
  "assetGroups": [
    {
      "name": "app",
      "installMode": "prefetch",
      "resources": {
        "files": [
          "/favicon.ico",
          "/index.html",
          "/*.css",
          "/*.js"
        ]
      }
    }
  ]
}
```

1. **Build the PWA**:

Run the following command to build your application for production:

```bash
Copy code
ng build --prod
```

2.4 Benefits of PWAs

- **Increased Engagement**: PWAs provide a better user experience, leading to higher engagement and retention.
- **Cross-Platform Compatibility**: PWAs work on any device with a modern web browser, reducing development costs for multiple platforms.
- **Reduced Development Time**: Instead of building separate applications for mobile and web, PWAs allow you to maintain a single codebase.

3. Microservices Architecture

3.1 Understanding Microservices

Microservices architecture is an approach to software development where applications are composed of small, independently deployable services that communicate over well-defined APIs. Each microservice is responsible for a specific business capability.

3.2 Advantages of Microservices

- **Scalability**: Individual services can be scaled independently based on demand, improving resource utilization.
- **Flexibility in Technology Stack**: Teams can choose different technologies for different services, allowing for optimization based on specific needs.
- **Improved Fault Isolation**: Issues in one microservice do not necessarily impact others, improving overall system resilience.

3.3 Implementing Microservices with ASP.NET Core

When building a microservices architecture with ASP.NET Core:

1. **Service Decomposition**: Break down your application into discrete services based on business capabilities.
2. **API Gateway**: Use an API Gateway (such as Ocelot) to route requests to the appropriate microservices, handle authentication, and aggregate responses.
3. **Service Communication**: Use lightweight communication protocols (like HTTP/REST or gRPC) to enable interaction between microservices.

Example of Setting Up Ocelot API Gateway

1. **Install Ocelot**:

```bash
bash
Copy code
dotnet add package Ocelot
```

1. **Configure Ocelot**: In ocelot.json, define the routing:

```json
json
Copy code
{
  "Routes": [
    {
      "DownstreamPathTemplate": "/api/products",
      "DownstreamScheme": "http",
```

```
"DownstreamHostAndPorts": [{ "Host": "products-service",
"Port": 80 }],
"UpstreamPathTemplate": "/products",
"UpstreamHttpMethod": [ "GET", "POST" ]
  }
 ]
}
```

1. **Configure Ocelot in Startup.cs**:

```csharp
Copy code
public void ConfigureServices(IServiceCollection services)
{
    services.AddOcelot();
}

public void Configure(IApplicationBuilder app,
IWebHostEnvironment env)
{
    app.UseOcelot().Wait();
}
```

3.4 Challenges of Microservices

While microservices offer many benefits, they also introduce complexity. Challenges include:

- **Distributed System Complexity**: Managing multiple services can lead to increased complexity in deployment and monitoring.
- **Data Management**: Each microservice may have its own database, requiring strategies for data consistency and integrity.
- **Inter-Service Communication**: Efficient communication between

services is essential, often requiring the implementation of message brokers like RabbitMQ or Kafka.

4. Serverless Computing

4.1 What is Serverless Computing?

Serverless computing allows developers to build and run applications without managing server infrastructure. In this model, the cloud provider dynamically allocates resources as needed, allowing for automatic scaling.

4.2 Advantages of Serverless Computing

- **Cost-Effectiveness**: You pay only for the resources consumed during execution, reducing costs compared to traditional server-based models.
- **Automatic Scaling**: Serverless architectures automatically scale up and down based on demand.
- **Focus on Development**: Developers can focus on writing code without worrying about server management.

4.3 Using Azure Functions for Serverless Applications

Azure Functions is a serverless compute service provided by Microsoft Azure. Here's how to implement it:

1. **Create a New Function**: Use the Azure Portal to create a new Azure Function App.
2. **Choose the Trigger**: Select the appropriate trigger (e.g., HTTP trigger, timer trigger) based on your use case.
3. **Write Your Function**: Implement your logic in the function. For example:

```csharp
Copy code
using Microsoft.AspNetCore.Mvc;
using Microsoft.Azure.WebJobs;
using Microsoft.Azure.WebJobs.Extensions.Http;
using Microsoft.AspNetCore.Http;
using Microsoft.Extensions.Logging;
using System.Threading.Tasks;

public static class GetProductsFunction
{
    [FunctionName("GetProducts")]
    public static async Task<IActionResult> Run(
        [HttpTrigger(AuthorizationLevel.Function, "get", Route =
        null)] HttpRequest req,
        ILogger log)
    {
        // Logic to get products
        return new OkObjectResult(products);
    }
}
```

4.4 When to Use Serverless

Serverless computing is ideal for:

- **Event-Driven Applications**: Applications that react to events (e.g., file uploads, API requests).
- **Microservices**: Building individual microservices that can scale independently.
- **Quick Prototyping**: Rapidly developing and deploying applications without infrastructure concerns.

5. API-First Development

5.1 What is API-First Development?

API-first development emphasizes designing and developing APIs before building the applications that consume them. This approach ensures that the API is well-defined and meets the needs of all stakeholders.

5.2 Advantages of API-First Development

- **Clear Contracts**: An API specification serves as a contract between front-end and back-end teams, reducing miscommunication.
- **Independent Development**: Front-end and back-end teams can work in parallel, speeding up the development process.
- **Improved Testing**: Well-defined APIs can be tested independently of the application, improving overall quality.

5.3 Implementing API-First Development

1. **Define API Specifications**: Use tools like **OpenAPI** (formerly Swagger) to define API endpoints, request/response formats, and authentication methods.
2. **Generate API Documentation**: Use OpenAPI to generate interactive documentation that serves as a reference for developers.
3. **Mock APIs**: Use tools like **Postman** or **Swagger UI** to create mock APIs for testing purposes before the actual implementation.

5.4 Best Practices

- **Versioning**: Implement API versioning to manage changes over time without breaking existing clients.
- **Rate Limiting**: Protect your API from abuse by implementing rate limiting to control the number of requests from users.

6. Continuous Integration and Continuous Deployment (CI/CD)

6.1 What is CI/CD?

CI/CD is a set of practices that enable development teams to deliver code changes more frequently and reliably. Continuous Integration (CI) involves automatically testing and integrating code changes into a shared repository. Continuous Deployment (CD) automates the deployment process to production.

6.2 Advantages of CI/CD

- **Faster Release Cycles**: CI/CD enables teams to release updates quickly and efficiently.
- **Increased Reliability**: Automated testing helps catch bugs early, improving overall application reliability.
- **Reduced Manual Work**: Automation reduces the burden on developers, allowing them to focus on writing code.

6.3 Setting Up CI/CD for Angular and ASP.NET Core

Using GitHub Actions for CI/CD

1. **Create a Workflow File**: In your GitHub repository, create a .github/workflows/ci-cd.yml file.

```yaml
Copy code
name: CI/CD Pipeline

on:
```

```
push:
  branches:
    - main

jobs:
  build:
    runs-on: ubuntu-latest

    steps:
      - name: Checkout code
        uses: actions/checkout@v2

      - name: Set up Node.js
        uses: actions/setup-node@v2
        with:
          node-version: '14'

      - name: Install dependencies
        run: npm install

      - name: Build Angular application
        run: ng build --prod

      - name: Run Angular tests
        run: npm test -- --watch=false

      - name: Publish ASP.NET Core application
        run: dotnet publish -c Release

      - name: Deploy to Azure
        run: az webapp deploy --name <app-name> --resource-group
        <resource-group-name> --src-path <path-to-publish>
```

Using Azure DevOps for CI/CD

1. **Create a New Pipeline**: In Azure DevOps, create a new pipeline and link it to your repository.
2. **Select the Build Template**: Choose templates for Angular and ASP.NET Core, and configure tasks for building, testing, and deploying

your applications.

6.4 Monitoring CI/CD Pipelines

Monitoring your CI/CD pipelines is essential for identifying issues and ensuring successful deployments. Use built-in tools in your CI/CD platform to track the status of builds, tests, and deployments.

7. The Future of Web Development

7.1 Evolving Technologies

Web development is continually evolving, with new frameworks, libraries, and tools emerging regularly. Staying informed about the latest technologies and trends will help you remain competitive in the industry.

7.2 Focus on User Experience

User experience will remain a critical focus in web development. Applications that prioritize usability, accessibility, and performance will continue to thrive in a competitive market.

7.3 Emphasis on Security

As cyber threats evolve, security will become increasingly important. Developers must prioritize secure coding practices, regular audits, and compliance with regulations to protect user data and application integrity.

7.4 Integration of AI and Machine Learning

Integrating AI and machine learning into web applications will become more common, enabling developers to create personalized experiences, enhance data analysis, and automate processes.

7.5 Community and Collaboration

The development community will continue to play a vital role in sharing knowledge, best practices, and tools. Participating in open-source projects, attending conferences, and engaging with peers can foster collaboration and innovation.

Conclusion

In this chapter, we explored advanced topics in full-stack development, including state management, Progressive Web Applications (PWAs), microservices, serverless computing, API-first development, and CI/CD practices. We also discussed future trends that will shape the landscape of web development.

By embracing these advanced concepts and staying informed about emerging technologies, you can enhance your skills as a full-stack developer and build applications that meet the evolving needs of users. As you continue your journey, remember that the key to success lies in continuous learning, adaptation, and a commitment to excellence.

This book has provided a comprehensive guide to building, maintaining, and optimizing full-stack applications with Angular and ASP.NET Core. With the knowledge and skills acquired, you are well-equipped to tackle new challenges and contribute to the exciting world of web development.

Chapter 15: The Journey of a Full-Stack Developer

Embarking on the journey to become a full-stack developer is both exciting and challenging. This chapter will discuss the personal and professional growth experienced on this path, the significance of community involvement, and the continuous pursuit of knowledge in web development. We will explore:

1. Defining Your Path as a Full-Stack Developer
2. Overcoming Challenges and Building Skills
3. The Importance of Community and Networking
4. Lifelong Learning and Professional Development
5. Crafting Your Portfolio and Personal Brand
6. Preparing for Future Opportunities
7. Reflections on Your Journey

By the end of this chapter, you will have a deeper understanding of the experiences that shape a successful full-stack developer and the mindset necessary for continuous growth in this dynamic field.

1. Defining Your Path as a Full-Stack Developer

1.1 Understanding the Role

A full-stack developer is a versatile professional skilled in both front-end and back-end development. This role requires a deep understanding of various technologies, languages, and frameworks, allowing developers to create complete web applications from conception to deployment.
  Key Responsibilities

- **Front-End Development**: Designing and implementing user interfaces using technologies like HTML, CSS, and JavaScript frameworks (e.g., Angular, React).
- **Back-End Development**: Building server-side logic, managing databases, and creating APIs using frameworks like ASP.NET Core or Node.js.
- **Collaboration**: Working with designers, product managers, and other stakeholders to deliver functional and visually appealing applications.

1.2 Identifying Your Interests and Strengths

To define your path, it's crucial to identify your interests and strengths within the full-stack development domain. Consider the following:

- **Front-End vs. Back-End**: Do you enjoy creating user interfaces and enhancing user experience, or are you more interested in server-side logic and database management?
- **Technological Preferences**: Are there specific programming languages or frameworks that you feel more comfortable with or passionate about?
- **Project Types**: What types of projects excite you? E-commerce platforms, content management systems, or social media applications?

By understanding your preferences, you can tailor your learning path and career trajectory to align with your passions.

2. Overcoming Challenges and Building Skills

2.1 Common Challenges Faced by Full-Stack Developers

The journey to becoming a proficient full-stack developer is filled with challenges, including:

- **Rapidly Changing Technologies**: The tech landscape is constantly evolving, making it difficult to keep up with new tools and frameworks.
- **Complex Problem Solving**: Full-stack development often involves solving complex technical problems that require deep knowledge and creativity.
- **Time Management**: Balancing learning, work, and personal projects can be challenging, especially for those new to the field.

2.2 Strategies for Overcoming Challenges

1. **Set Realistic Goals**: Break down your learning objectives into manageable tasks. Focus on mastering one technology or framework at a time.
2. **Embrace Continuous Learning**: Stay informed about industry trends and emerging technologies. Online courses, tutorials, and tech blogs can help you keep your skills sharp.
3. **Practice Regularly**: Build personal projects to apply what you've learned. Real-world application is crucial for reinforcing knowledge and gaining confidence.

2.3 Building Essential Skills

To succeed as a full-stack developer, focus on building the following skills:

- **Technical Skills**: Master programming languages (JavaScript, C#), frameworks (Angular, ASP.NET Core), and tools (Git, Docker).
- **Problem-Solving Skills**: Develop analytical thinking and the ability to troubleshoot issues efficiently.
- **Soft Skills**: Enhance communication, teamwork, and collaboration skills, which are vital in a development environment.

3. The Importance of Community and Networking

3.1 Engaging with the Developer Community

Being part of a community can significantly enhance your learning and growth as a developer. Engaging with others in the field provides opportunities to share knowledge, seek help, and build connections.

3.2 Benefits of Networking

1. **Knowledge Sharing**: Communities provide platforms for sharing resources, best practices, and insights. Participate in forums, discussion groups, and social media platforms like Twitter and LinkedIn.
2. **Mentorship Opportunities**: Connecting with experienced developers can provide invaluable guidance and support as you navigate your career.
3. **Job Opportunities**: Many job openings are filled through referrals within professional networks. Building relationships in the community can lead to potential job opportunities.

3.3 Ways to Get Involved

1. **Attend Meetups and Conferences**: Participate in local meetups and industry conferences to connect with fellow developers and learn about the latest trends.
2. **Contribute to Open Source**: Engaging with open-source projects allows you to collaborate with others, improve your coding skills, and showcase your work to potential employers.
3. **Join Online Communities**: Participate in online forums, Discord servers, or Slack groups dedicated to development topics.

4. Lifelong Learning and Professional Development

4.1 Embracing a Growth Mindset

A growth mindset is essential for continuous learning and professional development. Embrace challenges, view failures as opportunities to learn, and remain curious about new technologies and practices.

4.2 Setting Up a Learning Plan

Creating a structured learning plan can help you stay focused and organized. Consider the following steps:

1. **Identify Learning Goals**: Set specific, measurable goals based on your interests and career aspirations.
2. **Choose Learning Resources**: Utilize a mix of online courses, tutorials, books, and documentation to diversify your learning.
3. **Schedule Regular Learning Sessions**: Dedicate time each week to learn and practice new skills, ensuring consistency in your development.

4.3 Exploring Advanced Topics

As you progress in your journey, consider exploring advanced topics to deepen your expertise:

- **Cloud Computing**: Learn about cloud platforms (AWS, Azure, Google Cloud) and how to deploy applications in cloud environments.
- **DevOps Practices**: Understand the principles of DevOps, including CI/CD, automation, and infrastructure as code.
- **Microservices and API Development**: Explore the design and implementation of microservices architectures and RESTful APIs.

5. Crafting Your Portfolio and Personal Brand

5.1 Importance of a Strong Portfolio

A well-crafted portfolio is essential for showcasing your skills and experiences to potential employers. It serves as a testament to your abilities and helps differentiate you from other candidates.

5.2 Building Your Portfolio

1. **Include Relevant Projects**: Feature projects that demonstrate your full-stack development skills. Highlight your contributions and the technologies used.
2. **Showcase Problem Solving**: Include case studies that explain the challenges faced, the solutions implemented, and the outcomes achieved.
3. **Create a Professional Website**: Develop a personal website to host your portfolio, resume, and blog. This serves as a platform to showcase your work and share your thoughts on industry topics.

5.3 Personal Branding

Your personal brand reflects your values, skills, and professional identity. Consider the following strategies:

- **Engage on Social Media**: Share insights, projects, and achievements on platforms like LinkedIn and Twitter. Engage with others in the community to build visibility.
- **Write Technical Blogs**: Start a blog to document your learning journey, share tutorials, and discuss industry trends. This positions you as a knowledgeable resource in your field.
- **Network Strategically**: Connect with professionals in your desired industry and seek mentorship opportunities to build relationships that can lead to career advancements.

6. Preparing for Future Opportunities

6.1 Staying Updated with Industry Trends

The technology landscape is constantly changing, and staying informed about emerging trends is crucial for future success. Follow industry leaders, subscribe to newsletters, and participate in online courses to stay current.

6.2 Emphasizing Adaptability

In a rapidly evolving field, adaptability is key. Be open to learning new languages, frameworks, and methodologies as they emerge. The ability to pivot and embrace change will set you apart as a developer.

6.3 Career Path Exploration

Consider various career paths available to full-stack developers:

- **Specialization**: Focus on becoming an expert in a specific area, such as front-end development, back-end development, or DevOps.
- **Technical Leadership**: Transition into roles such as tech lead, architect, or engineering manager, where you guide development teams and influence technical decisions.
- **Consulting or Freelancing**: Explore opportunities as a consultant or freelancer, allowing you to work on diverse projects and develop a broad skill set.

7. Reflections on Your Journey

7.1 Celebrating Milestones

Take time to celebrate your achievements and milestones along your journey. Acknowledge the skills you've acquired, the challenges you've overcome, and the progress you've made.

7.2 Embracing Continuous Improvement

Understand that the journey of a developer is ongoing. Embrace continuous improvement and be proactive in seeking feedback, refining your skills, and evolving as a professional.

7.3 Giving Back to the Community

As you advance in your career, consider giving back to the community by mentoring junior developers, contributing to open-source projects, or sharing your knowledge through blogs and presentations.

Conclusion

The journey to becoming a full-stack developer is filled with challenges, opportunities, and continuous growth. By embracing a growth mindset, engaging with the community, and committing to lifelong learning, you can thrive in this dynamic field. As you navigate your career, remember the importance

Conclusion: The Journey of Building Full-Stack Applications

As we conclude this comprehensive exploration of full-stack development using Angular and ASP.NET Core, it is essential to reflect on the knowledge, skills, and best practices discussed throughout the book. The landscape of web development is constantly evolving, and as developers, we must remain adaptable, embrace new technologies, and prioritize user needs in our applications.

In this conclusion, we will summarize the key themes of the book, highlight the significance of continuous learning and community engagement, and provide final thoughts on becoming a successful full-stack developer.

1. Key Themes and Insights

1.1 The Power of Full-Stack Development

Full-stack development combines front-end and back-end technologies, enabling developers to build complete applications that meet user needs from start to finish. By mastering both areas, developers can create dynamic, interactive, and efficient applications that enhance user experiences.

1.1.1 Versatility and Flexibility

A full-stack developer possesses the versatility to work across various layers of an application. This flexibility allows for smoother collaboration with team members and a more profound understanding of the entire application architecture. With the knowledge of both Angular for front-end and ASP.NET Core for back-end, developers can effectively design and implement solutions that address complex business challenges.

1.2 Emphasis on User Experience

Throughout the book, we emphasized the importance of user experience (UX) in application development. A successful application not only meets functional requirements but also provides a seamless and enjoyable user experience.

1.2.1 User-Centric Design Principles

Implementing user-centric design principles involves understanding user needs, preferences, and pain points. By gathering feedback, conducting user testing, and analyzing user behavior, developers can make informed design decisions that enhance usability and engagement.

1.3 Performance Optimization

Performance optimization is a critical aspect of full-stack development. Slow-loading applications lead to user frustration and can negatively impact engagement and retention.

1.3.1 Techniques for Optimization

We explored various techniques for optimizing both front-end and back-end performance, including lazy loading, caching, efficient database queries, and code splitting. By applying these techniques, developers can ensure that their applications remain responsive and efficient, even under heavy load.

1.4 Continuous Learning and Adaptability

The world of technology is ever-changing, with new frameworks, libraries, and best practices emerging regularly. As developers, embracing a mindset of continuous learning is essential for staying relevant and effective in our roles.

1.4.1 Lifelong Learning

We discussed the importance of setting up a learning plan, seeking out educational resources, and engaging with communities. Lifelong learning enables developers to acquire new skills, adapt to changing trends, and remain competitive in the job market.

2. Community Engagement and Networking

2.1 The Value of Community

Engaging with the development community is crucial for personal and professional growth. Building connections with other developers allows for knowledge sharing, collaboration, and support.

2.1.1 Opportunities for Involvement

Participating in local meetups, online forums, and open-source projects can significantly enhance your learning experience. By exchanging ideas and experiences with peers, you can gain new perspectives, learn from others' successes and failures, and build lasting relationships.

2.2 Mentorship and Giving Back

As you progress in your career, consider seeking out mentors who can guide you through challenges and help you navigate your professional journey. Likewise, giving back to the community by mentoring others or contributing to open-source projects fosters a culture of collaboration and continuous improvement.

3. Final Thoughts on Becoming a Full-Stack Developer

3.1 Embracing Challenges

The journey to becoming a full-stack developer is filled with challenges, but each challenge presents an opportunity for growth and learning. Embrace these challenges as a natural part of the development process and view them as opportunities to enhance your skills.

3.2 Crafting Your Professional Identity

As you gain experience, focus on crafting your professional identity. Building a strong portfolio, engaging with the community, and sharing your knowledge through blogs or talks can help establish your brand as a skilled developer.

3.3 Looking Ahead

The future of web development is bright, with exciting advancements on the horizon. From serverless computing and microservices architecture to the integration of artificial intelligence, the possibilities are vast. Stay curious, remain adaptable, and be ready to embrace new technologies and methodologies as they emerge.

4. Conclusion

In conclusion, this book has provided a comprehensive guide to building and maintaining full-stack applications with Angular and ASP.NET Core. We have explored the intricacies of both front-end and back-end development, performance optimization techniques, best practices for security and maintenance, and the importance of community engagement.

As you embark on your journey as a full-stack developer, remember that the key to success lies in continuous learning, collaboration, and a relentless pursuit of excellence. By focusing on user experience, embracing new technologies, and engaging with the community, you can create impactful applications that resonate with users and drive business success.

May your journey in the world of full-stack development be filled with growth, discovery, and the joy of building applications that make a difference.